Donated by
Ian Thomson

Not for loan

A Decade Beyond Maastricht: The European Social Dialogue Revisited

Studies in Employment and Social Policy

Volume 25.

The titles published in this series are listed at the end of this volume

Studies in Employment and Social Policy

A Decade Beyond Maastricht: The European Social Dialogue Revisited

Edited by

Marc De Vos

KLUWER LAW INTERNATIONAL
THE HAGUE / LONDON / NEW YORK

Published by:
Kluwer Law International
P.O. Box 85889, 2508 CN The Hague, The Netherlands
sales@kluwerlaw.com
http://www.kluwerlaw.com

Sold and Distributed in North, Central and South America by:
Aspen Publishers, Inc.
7201 McKinney Circle, Frederick, MD 21704, USA

Sold and Distributed in all other countries by:
Turpin Distribution Services Limited
Blackhorse Road, Letchworth, Herts.,
SG6 1HN, United Kingdom

A C.I.P Catalogue record for this book is available from the Library of Congress.

Printed on acid-free paper.

ISBN 90-411-2163-3

Printed and bound in Great Britain by MPG Books Limited, Bodmin, Cornwall

Contents

The Authors

Wilfried Beirnaert holds a doctorate in law and a licenciate in political and social studies (University of Leuven 1960–1962). He is honorary director general of the Federation of Belgian Companies, where he is responsible for social questions. Since 1998, he has represented the Federation in the European Economic and Social Committee, where he serves as vice-chairman of the social section. He chairs the social affairs committee of UNICE for the period of 2000–2004. WB@vbo-feb.be

Penny Clarke is an adviser at the ETUC and assistant to the Deputy General Secretary, Jean Lapeyre. She works on social dialogue and collective bargaining issues. pclarke@etuc.org-www.etuc.org

Olaf Deinert, Doctor in Law (University of Rostock, 1998), is an assistant lecturer and researcher at Rostock University Law School and a member of the Institute for Labour Law and of the Institute for International Law at this University. He teaches labour law and civil law. In these fields and moreover in the field of social law he has published several research articles and presented several reports, especially on problems of international law. olaf.deinert@jurfak.uni-rostock.de

Marc De Vos holds a Licentiate and Doctorate in Law (University of Ghent, 1993 and 2000), a Master in Social Law (Université Libre de Bruxelles, 1994), and a Master of Laws (Harvard University, 2000). He is a professor at the Ghent University Law School, where he teaches courses on Belgian, European and international employment and labour law. In these and in related fields he has published, taught, and lectured extensively, both nationally and internationally, and in both academic and professional circles. Marc.DeVos@UGent.be; www.law.UGent.be/social

Filip Dorssemont holds a Licentiate and Doctorate in Law (University of Antwerp (UIA), 1993 and 2001), a Bachelor in Philosophy (Antwerp University (UFSIA), 1990) and a Master (Getuigschrift Aanvullende Studie) in Philosophy (University of Leuven, HIW, 1994). He is researcher at the Centre for the Enforcement of European Law at Utrecht University and part-time professor of Labour Law at Antwerp University. The author has published on subjects of collective labour law, fundamental workers' rights and Community employment law. F.dorssemont@law.uu.nl

Michèle Thozet has a degree in law and a diploma in political science from the University of Lyon. She has been working at the European Commission since 1973, first in the Secretariat-general, and then since 1989 in different areas of the DG Employment and Social Affairs: Equal Opportunities between men and women, Family Policy, European Social Fund, and European Social Dialogue. She is currently working on the EQUAL European Initiative in the European Social Fund. Michele.Thozet @cec.eu.int

Anne Van Lancker holds degrees in sociology (1978) and in social law (1987). A former researcher, university lecturer, and head of cabinet with Flemish ministers of employment and social affairs, she is an MEP (PSE group) while holding executive positions for the Belgian socialist party (SPa). As MEP, she is a member of several parliamentary committees including the Committee on Employment and Social Affairs. avanlancker@ europarl.eu.int

Part One
The Legal Framework

Chapter One
Some Reflections on the Origin, Problems and Perspectives of the European Social Dialogue[1]

Filip Dorssemont

SECTION I. SOCIAL PARTNERS AND COMMUNITY LAW, A TWOFOLD RELATIONSHIP

1. The relationship between social partners and Community law is twofold.

Social partners have been involved in the establishment of Community *social policy*. Furthermore, *Community law* has affected the functioning of the social partners *within the Community*.

§ 1. Consultation and Social Dialogue

2. The social partners have an impact on European social policy through a process of *consultation* and *social dialogue*.[2]

Right from the start of the Community, the social partners have been involved in advisory bodies established on the basis of the EC Treaty or on the basis of decisions of the Commission or the Council. Some consultations have taken place on an informal or less institutionalized basis. These committees are set up at various levels (sectorial, cross-sectorial), and might

---

[1] The author is indebted to Peter Morris, for the excellent care he took in linguistically revising an earlier draft of this contribution. Remaining errors of a linguistic nature are the sole responsibility of the author of the present contribution.

[2] The distinction between *consultation* and *social dialogue* is new speech. In industrial relations it is customary to oppose *consultation* with *collective bargaining*. They refer to two distinct patterns or models of workers' involvement at plant level. *Consultation* tends to affect the unilateral exercise of managerial prerogative in a formal or procedural way. *Collective bargaining* touches upon matters which *per se* cease to fall within the scope of a unilateral managerial prerogative.

Matters covered by collective bargaining can only be arranged and re-arranged on the basis of mutual consent. The term '(information and) consultation' traditionally refers to a bi-partite context of industrial relations. The term 'consultation' under article 138 and 139 EC Treaty refers to a *tri*partite context of industrial relations.

include representatives of the social partners organized at the national and/or at the Community level. They were conceived in order to deliver opinions to Community institutions at the latter's request or on a more spontaneous basis.[3]

These consultations *of*, rather than *between* management and labour pretend to serve a process of social policy and legislation *enacted* by Community institutions. The *consultation* has an auxiliary character. The process amounts, for example, to *joint opinions* or *recommendations* preceding Community directives.

According to the EC Treaty *social dialogue*[4] is to be distinguished from *consultation*. The focus seems to shift in an almost *Copernican* manner. The action of the social partners *at the Community level* is *presented* in its own right. The Community instruments appear to have an *auxiliary character*. Community intervention serves to *implement* agreements concluded at the Community level. The social dialogue amounts to European collective agreements, *implemented* for example by a Community Directive.

Prima facie, the *distinction* between 'consultation' and 'dialogue' (articles 138 and 139 EC Treaty) is reminiscent of the distinction in article 6 European Social Charter. Article 6 § 1 deals with 'joint consultation between workers and employers'. Article 6 § 2 deals with 'negotiation with a view to the conclusion of collective agreements'. Unfortunately, both categories are conceived of as variations on the theme of *collective bargaining*.[5] Similar wording does not amount to a similar distinction. According to the European Committee on Social Rights 'joined consultation' does not refer to a *tri*partite form of consultation by the government.[6] This *tri*partite character seems to be paramount in the drafting of the EC Treaty.

---

[3] See COM (98) 322, *Adapting and promoting the Social Dialogue at Community level*, pp. 6–9; COM (2002) 341 final, *The European Social Dialogue, a force for innovation and change*, 8–9 (The fact that the consultation procedure is being mentioned in documents regarding the *Social Dialogue*, undermines the idea that consultation and dialogue constitute two distinct, let alone separate chapters. Furthermore, the historical origin of the European Social Dialogue, the *Val Duchesse Dialogue*, confirms this impression); C. Barnard, *EC Employment Law*, Oxford, University Press, 2000, 559–567; D. Gadbin, "L'association des partenaires économiques et sociaux organisés aux procédures de décision en droit communautaire", (2000) *Rev. trim. D.E.*, 4–16; E. Franssen, *Legal Aspects of the European Social Dialogue*, Antwerpen, Intersentia, 2002, 49–59.

[4] See in this respect the distinction being made between *consultation* and *dialogue* in article 138 TEC.

[5] See the *rubrica* 'the right to bargain collectively' preceding article 6 of the European Social Charter.

[6] X, *The right to organise and to bargain collectively*, Strasbourg, Council of Europe Publishing, 2001, p. 50, nr. 136.

§ 2. Impact of Community Law on the Social Partners

3. The impact of Community Law on the functioning of the social partners is not to be underestimated either. The impact has been beneficial as well as disadvantageous. Organizations of workers tend to further and defend workers' interests. The Community legislator's promotion of workers' involvement provides a crucial means to realize that goal. Over the past decades the Community legislator has shown a preference for a particular form of workers' involvement,[7] a right to information and/or consultation.[8]

The legislator was far from reluctant to tackle information and consultation procedures that took place within the boundaries of one Member State only.[9]

Scrutinized from an ideological point of view, many directives relating to information and consultation tend to stress the sacrosanct *spirit of co-operation* between management and labour.[10]

The old spectre of communism haunting Europe should finally be defeated by a spirit of co-operation. The option of the Community legislator to substitute the formerly used 'spirit of *collaboration*' with the spirit of co-operation needs to be saluted. The term *co-operation* has been less subject to corporatist connotations.[11]

4. These directives will be *beneficial* for the influence of workers' organizations in so far as they are successful in occupying the seats of workers' representatives, exercising the right to information and consultation. The Community legislator is reluctant to tackle the question of the *identity* of workers' representatives. In general, the matter is delegated to the Member States. In this respect it is useful to reiterate the principle stated by article

---

[7] *Workers' involvement*: The term 'involvement' has been introduced into EC Employment Law due to article 2 h) Directive 2001/86. For an analysis: F. DORSSEMONT, "La directive 2001/86 du 8 octobre 2001 complétant le statut de la société européenne pour ce qui concerne l'implication des travailleurs", (16 April 2002) *Petites Affiches*, nr. 76, 38–39.

[8] See in chronological order: Directive 75/129 (Collective redundancy), Directive 77/187 (Transfer of undertakings), 94/45 (European Works Councils), Directive 2001/86 (Workers' involvement-European Company); Directive 2002/14 (Information and Consultation),

[9] See in this respect the Directives 75/129, 77/187 and 2002/14. These directives do not *per se* relate to cross-border information and consultation.

[10] See for example articles 6 and 9 Directive 94/45; article 4 and 9 Directive 2001/86; article 1 Directive 2002/14.

[11] The word '*collaborazione*' has been introduced by the *Codice civile* (1942) to describe the employment relation between an employer and employee under the fascist rule of Benito Mussolini. (Cf. Artcile 2086 of the Italian *Codice civile*. See furthermore, the *rubrica* of Section II of Capo I; Titolo II, Libro V).

5 of ILO Convention nr. 135: 'The existence of elected representatives cannot be used as a means to undermine the position of trade unions concerned'.

The directives can be construed as imposing an obligation on Member States to guarantee some kind of workers' representation.[12] They cannot be construed as approving or prohibiting a privileged form of workers' representation.

The latest EWC, SE, INFO CONS Directives[13] tend to work as a *catalyst* for *collective bargaining* at *plant* and group level. A characteristic of both the EWC and SE directive is the facility being offered to model a system of information and consultation in an enterprise or a group at the Community level, or to model workers' involvement according to the wishes of management and labour concerned. Though workers' organizations seem to have a historical vocation to engage in such a process, the identity of the workers' representatives within a so-called *special negotiating body* and their designation is relegated to the legislation and the practices of the Member States.[14]

Directive 2002/14 is somewhat different. The directive is more reluctant to choose between a statutory and a conventional way of shaping workers' involvement. It will be up to the Member States to decide whether information and consultation at plant level will have a statutory rather than a conventional basis. Whereas the former EWC and SE directives allow *elected representatives* within a so-called special negotiating body to act as a substitute for a trade union in a process of collective bargaining, Directive 2002/14 adheres to the category of 'social partners'.[15] Unfortunately, this category has not been defined. In view of the deeply rooted traditions of industrial relations it seems unlikely that the wording refers to an elected body of workers' representatives.

5. Article 137 EC Treaty recognized the possibility of implementing the Social Policy Directives through *transpositional* collective bargaining between management and labour.[16] In practice, the option for transpositional bargaining presupposes the existence of national and cross-sectorial collective bargaining.

---

[12] See Court of Justice, Case C-382/92 and Case C-383/92, *Commission* v. *UK*.

[13] Directives 94/45, 2001/86 and 2002/14.

[14] Article 5.2.a) Directive 94/45 and Article 3.2.b) Directive 2001/86.

[15] Article 5 Directive 2002/14.

[16] The article reiterates the principle laid down in article 2.4 of the Agreement on Social Policy. As pointed out by OJEDA-AVILLES the option for transpositional agreements can be traced back to the previous Directives 91/533; 92/56 and 92/84 as well as to article 28 of the Community Charter of Fundamental Social Rights. See A. ADINOLFI, "The implementation of Social Policy Directives through Collective Agreements?", (1988) *C.M.L.R.*, 291–316; A. LYON-CAEN, "Le rôle des partenaires sociaux

Council Directive 93/104, concerning certain aspects of the organization of working time, is different from the approach of the Information and Consultation Directive and from article 137.4 EC Treaty. Instead of allowing Member States to recognise collective bargaining as a valid alternative to statutory intervention, it stresses the subsidiary character of State intervention. Article 4 of the Directive 93/104 seems to reverse the classic hierarchy between law and collective bargaining within the Member States.

6. Obviously the recorded hierarchy of norms also constitutes a limit to collective bargaining.[17] Social Partners are supposed to respect Community law while drafting collective agreements. Directive 75 117 (equal remuneration) obliges Member States to take all necessary measures to guarantee that clauses of collective agreements which are at odds with the principle of equal remuneration are void, can be declared void or can be amended.[18]

7. Since collective agreements should be compatible with Community law, the question arises whether the *conclusion* of collective agreements is not by its very nature at odds with the principle of *free competition.*

8. The question of whether *national* collective agreements are at odds with the principle of free competition might touch upon a *taboo* subject or might be a *delicate* issue; it is far from being absurd.[19]

Collective agreements tend to regulate working conditions on the *labour market*.

The collective agreement tends to eliminate *social* competition by workers willing to offer their services at a lower price than that preferred by the unionized workers. Eliminating social competition is not just a consequence or an effect of collective agreements; it is the quintessence or the *ratio legis*. The obligation not to disturb social peace or to maintain *social peace* was the counterpart paid by the unions.

9. In former times *craftsmen* tried to ensure high wages by limiting free

---

dans la mise en oeuvre du droit communautaire", (1997) *Droit social*, 74; A. Ojeda-Aviles, "European Collective Bargaining: A triumph of the Will?", *IJCLLIR*, 1993, 287–288.

[17] See N. Aliprantis, *La place de la convention collective dans la hiërarchie des normes*, Paris, LGDJ, 1980, 92–94.

[18] See article 4 Directive 75/117. Recent anti-discrimination directives contain similar clauses (See article 14 b) Directive 2000/43 and article 16 b) Directive 2000/78)

[19] See for example the fact that in ninenteenth-century Belgian law and legal doctrine, limitations on the freedom of enterprise of workers *and* employers were were considered to be a violation of the 'liberté du travail', synonymous with the 'liberté de l'industrie'. E. Haus, *Des coalitions industrielles et commerciales*, Gent, H. Hoste, 1862, 458 p. and

access to the labour market. Since highly qualified 'journeymen' (French: 'compagnons') played a key role in offering training to new apprentices, a *numerus clausus* was easily enforced. If an employer wanted to hire workers willing to accept lower wages, these 'journeymen' could respond by boycotting the employers or by refusing to offer training to the apprentices.[20] They would choose collective dismissal or would persuade their members not to work for the employer concerned.

The modern trade union consisting of less qualified workers have preferred strike action *rather* than a boycott in order to force an employer to accept wage increases. Rather than preventing access to the labour market, they would directly control or impose working conditions. Social competition may be prevented even further beyond the scope of the affiliates to the signatory parties by the State legislation and/or policies, thus generalizing the scope of a collective agreement.

10. The question of whether *European* collective agreements are at odds with the principle of free competition has basically become irrelevant. The legitimacy of *European* collective agreements has been 'consecrated' and favoured by the EC Treaty itself. It might be a particular disposition conceptually at odds with the principle of free competition. However, *lex specialis* as well as *lex posterior derogat priori.* The vision of the Court of Justice granting an 'immunity' to *collective agreements concluded within the Member States, subject to ratione materiae conditions,* was based on a logical reference *per analogiam* to the articles relating to European collective agreements.[21]

11. The question of whether systems of collective bargaining developed in a spontaneous order and supported by State legislation are compatible with EC principles of free competition might be regarded as extremely shocking for anyone who strongly supports fundamental (human) rights.

C.F. Waelbroeck, *De la liberté des coalitions industrielles et commerciales*, Brussel, A. Lacroix, 1867, 152 p.

[20] For a general survey, see E. Coornaert, *Les compagnonnages*, Paris; Les Editions ouvrières, 1966, 435 p.; C. Lis and H. Soly, "An irresistible Phalanx: Journeymen Associations in Western Europe, 1300–1800", in C. Lis, J. Lucassen and H. Soly, *Before the Unions*, (*International review of Social History*), 1994, 11–52; E. Martin Saint-Leon, *Le compagnonnage*, Paris, Librairie Armand Collin, 1901, 374 p. For a well documented 'case' of a collective action by 'journeymen' (compagnons): C. Lis and H. Soly, "De macht van 'vrije arbeiders'/collectieve acties van hoedenmakersgezellen in de Zuidelijke Nederlanden (zestiende eeuw- negentiende eeuw)", in C. Lis and H. Soly, *Werken volgens de regels*, Brussel, Vubpress, 1994, 15–50.

[21] Court of Justice, 21 September 1999, Case C-67/96, Albany International BV v. Stichting Bedrijfsfonds Textielindustrie.

Collective agreements constitute a spontaneous and natural outcome of the recognition of three fundamental workers' rights:

(a) the freedom of association, the right to form and join trade unions
(b) the right to strike
(c) the right to or freedom of collective bargaining.[22]

Although *free competition* is obviously a driving force and even a legal principle of the Community's economy, it has never achieved the status of a *human right* in any internationally binding legal human rights instruments. It seems extremely difficult to confer to it the status of a civil, political or even social or economic right. The freedom of enterprise was the object of constitutional recognition in some Member States such as France, Italy and Germany. The recognition should be understood as an antithesis to an extremely detrimental and state-authoritarian *species* of fascist corporatism.[23] Furthermore, it is obvious from these constitutions that the freedom of enterprise had a functional character. The exercise of the freedom of enterprise was subject to public utility. The recognition of the freedom of enterprise as a fundamental right in the Nice *Charter of Fundamental Rights* is nothing more than a historical error and an anomaly.

The idea that national collective agreements would be incompatible *with* the principle of free competition as guaranteed by articles 81 and 82 EC Treaty would have implied an *open conflict* with the standards and even the basic *constitutional* principles of the International Labour Organization. The right of collective bargaining is mentioned in Part III of the Declaration concerning the aims and purposes of the *International Labour Organization.* An approach that sees the *labour market* as being subject to the rules of *free competition* finally boils down to the reduction of *labour* to a *commodity.*[24] The idea that *labour is not a commodity* is not just a pleasant dream,

[22] This idea is implicitly put forward by many authors (O. Deinert, *Der europäische Kollektivvertrag*, Baden-Baden, Nomos Verlaggesellschaft, 1999, 254–270 (with regard to 'Kollektivvertragautonomie'); E. Franssen, n. 3 above, at 16–27; A. Jacobs, "Het recht op collectief onderhandelen in rechtsvergelijkend en Europees perspectief", Alphen aan den Rijn,, Samson, H.D. Tjeenk Willink, 1986, 388–395; A. Lo Faro, *Regulating Social Europe, Oxford, Portland Oregon*, 2000, 92–103 (with regard to *freedom of association*)), who wonders whether these fundamental human rights are granted at all at Community level. The question is crucial to the assessment of whether an appropriate conceptual framework exists in order to construe ECAs as *collective agreements.*

[23] See F. Dorssemont, "Sire laat de Staat de straat respecteren. Over fundamentele werknemersrechten en democratie", in B. Hubeau and M. Elst, *Democratie in ademnood? Over legitimiteit, legitimatie en verfijning van de democratie*, Brugge, Die Keure, 2002, 310–313.

[24] See in this respect the clearcut statement of Ichino that 'the safeguard of competition holds constitutional relevance only with reference to goods, services and capital market; it is not applicable to the labour market, where only the free movement of workers, but

neither is it a pathetic and oral exhortation. It constitutes the hard core of the *Declaration of Philadelphia.*

Since these principles chronologically stem from the previous ILO Constitution, a Member State is always able to invoke these obligations in order to justify its departure from an interpretation of articles 81 and 82 of the EC Treaty.[25]

12. The fact that practices and legislation guaranteeing fundamental human rights can be and are being challenged on the basis of purely economic principles has necessitated that the Court of Justice be extremely creative in referring to general programmatic clauses of the EC Treaty, lacking more clear-cut, explicit and authoritative proclamations of economic and social rights. Laying down these fundamental human rights is a pressing need. Such an exercise will obviously be useless, if some legal principles of the economic order are given the status of fundamental human rights. The neutral juxtaposition of purely economic principles and classic fundamental human rights within one Charter will not be sufficient to solve the crucial political and moral question of whether purely economic interests should *per se* prevail over social and economic rights or fundamental human rights.

13. Furthermore, an identification of collective agreements as an agreement between undertakings would have implied an assimilation of workers' organizations as signatory parties with an *undertaking*. The Court's disqualification of collective agreements aimed at the improvement of working conditions as distorting agreements in the sense of article 81 EC Treaty was based on an analysis *ratione materiae* of the article concerned. An analysis *ratione personae* might have been another way in which to disregard article 81.[26]

The recent BECU-case[27] is a striking example of how to resolve an

---

not the free competition among them is protected'. P. ICHINO, "Collective Bargaining and Antitrust Laws: an Open Issue", (2001) *IJCLLIR*, 189.

[25] Cf Article 307 EC Treaty and Court of Justice, 2 August 1993, C-158/91, Ministère public et Direction du Travail et de l 'emploi contre Jean-Claude Levy.

[26] See in this respect the observations made by A.M. VAN DEN BOSSCHE, "CAO's en mededingingsrecht", in M. RIGAUX, *Actuele Problemen van het Arbeidsrecht 6*, Antwerpen, Intersentia, 2001, p. 706, nr. 60; E.M.H. LOOZEN, "CAO's, bedrijfspensioenfondsen en het EG-mededingingsrecht", (1999) *Nederlands Tijdschrift voor Europees recht*, 281–282; K.J.M. MORTELMANS, "Vloeken in de kerk: de nieuwe economische Mededingingswet, toepasbaar op overeenkomsten op de arbeidsmarkt", (1998) *Sociaal Recht*, 252–253; M. PALLINI, "Il rapporto problematico tra diritto della concorrrenza e autonomia collettiva nell'ordinamento communitario e nazionale", (2000) *Rivista italiana del diritto del lavoro*, II, 238–241.

[27] Court of Justice, 16 September 1999, Case C-22/98.

apparent conflict between EC Competition law and the necessity for specific social protection of the port workers. In the BECU Case, the Belgian law providing for social protection of harbour workers through a limitation of the access to the labour market was challenged on the basis of the principles of free competition. The harbour workers who were recognized to perform harbour works were explicitly disregarded as undertakings within the meaning of article 81 EC Treaty. Paramount was the observation that workers even taken collectively could not qualify as an undertaking, since they were incorporated into the undertakings concerned.

Trade unions can be construed as enterprises from the labour lawyers' point of view. They tend to conclude labour contracts as employers. The crucial question at stake is whether they can be considered as enterprises from a commercial law point of view. They should therefore produce services or goods, which affect the common market.

Section II. On the Origins of Collective Bargaining at Community Level: A Source of Conceptual and Legal Problems?

§ 1. Ceci n'est pas une Convention Collective Européenne?

14. The question arises whether European (collective) agreements can be construed as *collective agreements.*

Is the wording appropriate or is it misleading? Does the legal term (*signifiant*) correspond with its conceptual meaning (*signifié*)?

The question starts from the assumption that the legal definition of the term 'collective agreement' is the object of a *communis opinio.* The EC Treaty fails to provide a proper definition of collective agreements. Article 139 EC Treaty tends to qualify agreements as a *species* of the *genus* 'contractual relations'. This approach is puzzling. It would have been closer to existing legal traditions to conceive of agreements as a *genus.* Agreements might be divided between agreements deprived of an *animus contrahendae obligationis*, so-called gentlemen's agreements, and those expressing a clear will to create legal obligations, i.e. collective contracts or conventions.

Some Member States have elaborated a legal framework to regulate and institutionalize collective bargaining. These legislations often define the object of collective agreements. It is fashionable to distinguish between the *normative* and the *obligatory* part of the collective agreement. Not all legal definitions refer to both parts, neither is it clear whether the obligatory part is a constitutive part of the collective agreement.[28]

[28] For legal definitions including a reference to a normative and obligatory part: Article 5 of the Belgian Act of December 1968 regarding collective industrial agreements and joint committees; § 2 of the German *Tarifvertragsgesetz.* The definition of a collective

ILO recommendation n° 91 defines collective agreements as 'agreements in writing regarding working conditions and terms of employment concluded between an employer or a group of employers or one or more employers' organizations and one or more employees' organizations'.[29]

It is noteworthy that such a definition does not contain any reference to the so-called *obligatory* part of the collective agreement. The latter is important, since it seems extremely difficult to deduce an explicit hard obligatory core in the European collective agreements concluded so far.

From a formal point of view European collective agreements seem to correspond to some of the legal definitions of collective agreements at the international and national level.

15. Conceptual problems regarding the legal construction and understanding of European collective agreements as collective agreements are due to other factors. The basic problem does not stem from a scholarly definition of the term 'collective agreements'.

The following three considerations seem more useful and important in explaining the unease or the speculation of legal scholars, while attempting to analyse the European collective agreement.

16. The relation between collective agreements at the Community level as a sociological *donné* and the legal construction (*construit*) seems radically different from that at the Member State level.

Historically, collective bargaining and collective agreements at Member State level developed in a *spontaneous* order. Their overall non-existence in the nineteenth century was the consequence of active State intervention, repressing the freedom of association, the right to collective action and the right to collective bargaining. The withdrawal of that repression made the emergence of collective bargaining at Member State level almost inevitable. The effective use of collective action was sufficient to fill the gap. The subsequent *legal construction* of a phenomenon rooted in a spontaneous and autonomous order took place in the context of increased democratization of national parliaments.

---

agreement according to Dutch law does not include a reference to an obligatory part (Cf Article 1 of the Dutch Law on Collective Agreements). Article 8 does contain an obligation upon signatories to influence their members. The sections of the French *Code du Travail* regarding the collective agreement do not contain any reference to the existence of an obligatory part.

[29] See in this respect E. FRANSSEN, n. 3 above, at 101–105. The bulk of ILO instruments deal with a definition of *collective bargaining*, rather than focusing on *collective agreements*.

17. LUYTEN,[30] a *connaisseur* of the genesis of the Belgian (projected) corporatist and actual neo-corporatist institutionalization of industrialized relations, explained the willingness of employers' organizations to accept collective bargaining at sectorial or cross-sectorial level as being due to the threat of legal intervention. BERCUSSON has explained the invention and the efficiency of the European social dialogue in similar terms as a process of collective bargaining *under the shadow of the law*.[31]

Two differences exist. The threat of legislation did not stem from a *parliamentary* legislator, nor from the recognition of universal suffrage. The threat of legislative intervention was closely linked to the extension of matters regulated by qualified majority rather than by unanimous decision of the Council.

18. The fact that European collective bargaining seems to have been provoked rather than merely institutionalized by Community institutions implies a risk of it being deprived of the checks and balances of a previous expression of *collective autonomy*. The division of the European economy into so-called sectorial branches or professions is a delicate exercise. In the past, Member States could take into account the formation of professional organizations in order to define the division of the economy into professions. Such a subjective approach tends to respect the spontaneous and autonomous identification by workers with 'their' branch or profession. Finally, the freedom of association and the right to organize are at stake. It is up to workers to decide with whom they want to unite and to be identified with at a professional level.

A more proactive and 'objective' attitude risks provoking unpleasant reminders of the 'ontological' approach of the profession, being a severely criticized characteristic of fascist industrial relations.[32]

19. Another structural 'conceptual' problem with the present state of collective bargaining at the Community level is the fact that Community law

---

[30] See D. LUYTEN, *Ideologisch debat en politieke strijd over het corporatisme tijdens het interbellum*, Brussel, KAWLSK, 1996, 13.

[31] B. BERCUSSON, "The Dynamic of European Labour Law after Maastricht", (1994) *Industrial Law Journal*, 20–22; B. BERCUSSON, "Maastricht: a fundamental change in European Labour Law", (1992) *Industrial Relations Journal*, 185; B. BERCUSSON, *European Labour Law*, London, Butterworths, 2000, 540. See furthermore the analogous observations from G. LYON-CAEN "Le droit social de la Communauté européenne après le Traité de Maastricht", (1993) *Recueil Dalloz Sirey*, 152: 'Si la Commission veut soutenir le processus de négociation, il faut qu'elle "terrorrise" les interlocuteurs sociaux par des projets de textes que les uns et (ou) les autres jugeront excessifs ou dangereux'.

[32] See G. GIUGNI, *Diritto sindacale*, Bari, Cacucci, 2000, 73–76; M. PERSIANI, *Diritto sindacale*, Padova, Cedam, 1999, 8–9.

lacks a clear-cut and explicit recognition of the *classic triptich of fundamental workers' rights.*

(a) the freedom of association
(b) the right to strike
(c) the right of collective bargaining.

The present viewpoint of Community law is one of reluctance and abstentionism.

This might be understood as a sign of profound respect for these fundamental workers' rights. Unfortunately, these rights need to be protected not just *against*, but also *through* public authority. The statement is particularly valid when practices and legal instruments of Member States reflecting social and economic rights are being scrutinized on the basis of economic legal principles.

20. Scholars differ in their opinions on the state of recognition of these rights in the Community legal order.[33] The actual timid and fragmentary recognition of these rights by the Court of Justice shows that these rights are being made subject to the assessment of a *gouvernement des juges.*

One might argue that in practice the recognition of the right to strike and the freedom of collective bargaining as fundamental workers' rights

[33] A. Lo Faro is extremely skeptical about the state of recognition of the freedom of association within the Community legal order. The author only contemplates the freedom of association, which in his view is not recognized as such within the Community legal order. Neither the freedom to collective bargaining nor the right to strike are the object of research. A. Lo Faro, n. 22 above, at 92–104.

Other authors share a more optimist approach. Franssen (E. Franssen, n. 3 above, at 16–27) concludes that two of the fundamental workers' rights of the classic tryptich have been recognized, on the basis of an analysis of the Case-Law of the Court of Justice. Only the right to strike is the object of absolute mutism by the Court. The author refers to the opinion of the Advocate General expressed in the *Albany* Case, stating that the freedom of collective bargaining can be reconstructed on the basis of the freedom to contract. Such a deduction is not entirely convincing. A collective agreement cannot be reduced to a collective exercise through mandate of the individual freedom to contract. Collective autonomy is autonomous *vis à vis* the freedom to contract. The fact that civil law and contract law were not suitable for a proper construction of the collective agreement has pushed many legislators to pass *leges speciales.* Furthermore, such a reconstruction tends to neglect the fact that collective agreements have a double nature, including an obligatory part and a normative part.

O. Deinert (n. 22 above, at 253–438) describes the recognition of the freedom of association and of collective bargaining as a legal principle and human right recognized by Community Law (*collective autonomy)* on the basis of a comprehensive comparative law research, including all the Member States. See furthermore, C. Barnard, *EC Employment Law*, Oxford, University Press, 551–577.

was preceded by the existence of collective agreements and even a legal framework regulating the effects thereof. The necessity of a Community framework of fundamental workers' rights for a proper legal construction of collective agreements does not need to be exaggerated. However, can this still be argued in a case when a comprehensive legal framework relating to collective agreements is lacking?

21. Whether or not the *right to strike* has been recognized by Community law, the fact remains that authentic cross-state collective actions of a revindicative rather than demonstrative character are *rari nantes.*

The idea that collective bargaining will take place *under the shadow of the law* might be a comfort to the trade unions involved in the negotiation. However, the shadow of the legislator tends to dissolve, once the bargaining process is finished. For an enforcement of the ECA in the spontaneous order of industrial relations the threat of industrial action seems to be vital. It is questionable whether such a threat is realistic.

22. Thirdly, the fact remains that in spite of the virtual opportunities created by articles 138 and 139 of the EC Treaty, the legal framework regarding European collective agreements provides an embryonic outlook. The articles of the EC Treaty tend to obscure rather than to enlighten. The harvest of collective agreements is poor in quantity and quality. The case-law on the interpretation of these articles has remained sparse. The *main* legal source on European collective bargaining is constituted by scholarly research which has a very speculative character.

23. According to a majority view, the binding of European collective bargaining seems to imply an *ad hoc* legal intervention of Community institutions or by the social partners and the legislators at Member State level. The difference with the scope *ratione personae* of *institutionalized* collective agreements at Member State level is striking. The binding effect of those agreements does not imply an *ad hoc* intervention. Some Member States have enacted laws providing that the normative part of collective agreements is automatically binding upon the workers and employers involved. Member States may differ whether the binding of employees requires membership of the signatory trade union or not. State intervention through the instrument of the *extension erga omnes* broadens the scope *ratione personae* of this binding. However, it does not *constitute* the binding as such.

The distinction between the *binding effect* and the *extension* of this binding is blurred by a unique and single implementation procedure.

24. A legal analysis of articles 138 and 139 EC Treaty amounts to the question of whether European collective agreements can be construed as being the outcome of some form of 'collective autonomy' at Community level. The question arises whether the pretended promotion of collective bargaining at Community level does not constitute a *fiction*. The legal fiction serves to hide the true *function* of its introduction within the EC Treaty.[34] ECAs are said to give support to Community regulation and legitimacy. The thesis defended by the distinguished scholar Lo Faro is not bereft of merits and arguments.

It goes without saying that the introduction of the ECAs took place during a period of regulatory deficiency. It has been promoted by Community institutions incapable of passing projected social policies. It is difficult to conceive of the introduction of ECAs in the EC Treaty as a classical 'reception' or (*exequatur*) by a supra-state order of an existing phenomenon generated by a so called infra-state legal order.

Lo Faro has argued that the necessary preconditions for the construction of ECAs as an expression of collective autonomy are absent.[35] Collective autonomy at the Community level presupposes a collective identity of workers at that level. Legal categories might be seen as an expression of such an identity. They can help to shape or confirm it. The invention of categories such as 'the employee' or ' the profession' at Member State level is an example. At present, the category of 'employee' can hardly be qualified as an autonomous category of Community law.

Furthermore, the recognition of collective autonomy within a classic legal pluralistic *paradigma* implies a fundamental legal framework recognizing freedom of association.

Alongside these negative indications Lo Faro points at positive indications refuting the idea that the Community legal order is willing to recognize the collective autonomy of the social partners. The transposition procedure of the European collective agreements through a Council decision on a proposal by the Commission implies a previous monitoring of the ECA which is at odds with respect for collective autonomy.

Lo Faro mentions the legality check, the control over the representative status, the need to assure the protection of the small and medium-sized enterprises. Furthermore, the Commission tends to assess explicitly the appropriateness of transposition while monitoring the ECA.[36] The choice

---

[34] See the revealing Italian title of Lo Faro's monography *Funzioni et Finzioni della contrattazione collettiva communitaria*, Milano, Giuffrè editore, 1999, 353 p.

[35] See A. Lo Faro, *Regulating Social Europe*, n. 22 above, at 65–89.

[36] See E. Franssen, n. 3 above, at 207–208.

of the Commission and the Council for a Directive implies a double transposition of the original act. The transposition of a directive is *per se* limited to the results of the envisaged directive. Apparently, it does not imply a literal recapitulation of the text *in extenso* of the ECA.

Lo Faro's assessment finally boils down to the conclusion that the distinction between Community directives preceded by consultation of management and labour and directives supposed to transpose European collective agreements is of a rhetorical nature.

25. It is beyond doubt that the legal construction and the subsequent *genesis* of European collective bargaining are essentially different from the *genesis* and the subsequent legal construction of national collective bargaining. Lo Faro's writings tend to demonstrate a clash between the role which Community public authority attributes in fact to the European social partners and the historic vocation of trade unions. The use of the wording 'European collective agreement' is *reminiscent* of the historical reality of factual industrial relations within the Member States. The latter differs radically from the genesis and the actual reality of industrial relations at the Community level.

Although both considerations seem to be valid, they do not seem sufficient to refute the use of the expression 'collective agreements' within the EC Treaty. The clash between the role attributed by public authority to trade unions and their autonomous and historical vocation is not specific to Community labour law at all. It has been a characteristic of the attitudes of any public authority right from the very beginning of the trade union movement. These clashes do not *per se* jeopardize the factual and political autonomy of the trade union movement.

On the other hand, the legal categories, although they might be reminiscent of sociological phenomena, tend to have a proper *autonomy*. Even though the development and the construction of ECAs may be rooted in historical realities which are different from that of collective agreements at Member State level, the future may prove that they tend to transcend this reality as well.

Furthermore, the legal categories of 'social dialogue' and 'European collective agreement' can be construed as autonomous concepts of Community law, which are not to be interpreted *per se* according to the traditions, the constitutional and legal traditions of Member States.

The vast majority of legal scholars implicitly refused to do so. Scholarly analysis of the ECA is moulded and drafted in the traditional categories and focuses on the traditional questions so common to collective agreements within Member States.

SECTION III. CONCEPTUAL AND LEGAL PROBLEMS

26. A critical analysis of articles 138 and 139 of the EC Treaty generates various legal and conceptual problems. A meta-juridical approach[37] to the introduction of the notion of 'European Collective Agreements' increases rather than solves these problems.

A comprehensive analysis of these problems exceeds the limits of this contribution. It goes beyond the imagination of scholars confronted with the analysis of a legal text regarding ECA which does not yet correspond to a rich harvest.

27. We will focus on four main problems.

The first concerns the identification of the actors within the European Social Dialogue under articles 138 and 139 EC Treaty. The second concerns the need to identify an obligatory part or a hard core of obligations for the signatory parties. The third question touches upon the question of the autonomy of the social partners and to what extent the Council and the Commission have to respect it. The fourth question revolves around the meaning of the term 'Council decision' in article 139 EC Treaty.

§ 1. 'Management and Labour'

28. *Title XI* on *Social Policy* refers to social partners in the most abstract way as 'management' and 'labour'. Articles 138 and 139 EC Treaty envisage the eventuality of 'agreements' between 'management and labour' as the outcome of a Social Dialogue at the community level.

The distinction between management and labour is unfortunate. From a legal point of view 'managers' are often bound by contracts of employment, thus being part of the workforce. The use of the word 'management' has two advantages. It consolidates managers' perception that they do not belong to the workforce. Furthermore, it avoids using the word 'capital' and 'labour', so reminiscent of an inconvenient discourse on class struggle. The notion of 'social partners' used in other versions[38] of the text is a source of further delight, joy and harmony.

The reference to 'management' and 'labour' is used on various and

---

[37] For a legal study not deprived of meta-juridical excursions, involving reflections on industrial relations, legal and political theory: A. LO FARO, *Regulating Social Europe*, Oxford, Portland Oregon, 2000, 192 pages and A. LO FARO, *Funzioni et Finzioni della contrattazione colletiva communitaria,* Milano, Giuffrè, 1999, 353 p.

[38] See for example the Dutch, French, Italian and German version of Article 138 EC Treaty.

extremely distinct occasions, generating legal effects which are extremely different in nature.

29. *'The Commission shall have the task to promote the consultation of management and labour and shall take any relevant measures to facilitate their dialogue'.*[39] The distinction between 'consultation' and 'dialogue' is far from clear. The ambiguity stems from the fact that 'joint consultation' can be construed as synonymous with social dialogue or even as an aspect of collective bargaining.[40] Furthermore, it can refer to consultation by public authorities in order to define, to shape and to legitimize their policies.

A specific *species* of consultation is a consultation concerning proposals in the social policy field. Article 138 EC Treaty provides two successive consultation procedures for management and labour. The Commission is forced to consult management and labour twice, if it persists in its wish to submit a proposal. On the occasion of the second consultation, management and labour have the opportunity to 'hijack'[41] the legislative powers of the Commission and the Council, by expressing their wish to initiate the process amounting to a European collective agreement.

Through the conclusion of a *European* collective agreement, the signatories empower the Council upon the proposal of the Commission to take a Decision implementing the agreement, generating legislation in the field of

---

[39] See Article 138 EC Treaty.

[40] See Article 6 of the European Social Charter.

[41] *To hijack:* Many legal scholars hold the idea that the process of collective bargaining *suspends* the powers of the Commission to submit the proposal. The limit to the duration of the bargaining procedure under article 138 4) EC Treaty would be meaningless, if such *a suspension* was not implied. See for example: L. Betten, "The role of social partners in the Community's social policy law-making: participatory democracy or furthering the interests of small elites", in C. Engels and M. Weiss, *Labour Law and Industrial Relations at the Turn of the Century*, London, Kluwer Law International, 1998, 250–251 (the author acknowledges that the thesis of non-suspension is purely theoretical and sticks to the term 'hijacking').

This legal effect has not been made explicit in article 138 EC Treaty. The article does not explicitly state that the Commission must await the outcome of the first and second consultation before submitting a proposal. Some scholars are more reluctant to assume that the social dialogue is capable of suspending and/or substituting the legislative powers of the Community institutions. See G. Guery, "La dimension conventionnelle de l'Europe sociale sur la base du Traité de Maastricht", (1992) *Revue internationale du Travail*, 638 (The author stresses that the legislative procedure is completely autonomous, irrespective of a consultation of social partners) and Ph. Langlois, "Europe sociale et principe de subsidiarité", (1993) *Droit social*, 207 ('Le dialogue social communautaire ne peut jamais prévaloir sur les pouvoirs institutionnels'). The author does however recognize that there is a case for a suspension of legislative power during the consultation process. (–, 205: 'paralysie forcée').

social policy. Thereby they tend to bypass the common institutional, i.e. parliamentary, checks and balances.

30. A great deal of scholarly debate has arisen ever since the judgement of the Tribunal of First Instance following the UEAPME decision to challenge the Parental Leave Directive.[42]

A balanced view of the subject of the representativeness of the social partners requires distinguishing the various competences attributed to representative social partners.

As far as consultation is deprived of legal effects, it seems difficult to imagine that public authorities would not be allowed to consult whoever they want to consult. The question arises whether the opposite is true. Does the Commission have the right *not* to consult certain organizations. Do *representative* social partners have a right to be consulted by public authorities in a legislative process which affects their interests?

In the *Affaire Syndicat National de la Police belge* the European Court of Human Rights decided that a right to be heard is part of the hard core of the freedom to constitute and join workers' organizations.[43]

31. The Commission took the opportunity of elucidating the principles governing the selection to be made between social partners in a series of communications.[44]

In a recommendation in 1993 the Commission stated the criteria for representativeness regarding the consultation procedure as such. It is remarkable that no distinction was made between the two stages of the consultation. Indeed, organizations deemed to be representative for the second stage have the capacity to hijack the Commission, thus delaying an institutional process of legislation.

The criteria show that the Commission seeks to stimulate the federation

---

[42] Court of First Instance, 17 June 1998, UEAPME, nr. T-135/96.

See: B. Bercusson, "Democratic Legitimacy and European Labour Law", (1999) *Industrial Law Journal*, 153–170; L. Betten, "The Democratic Deficit of Participatory Democracy in Community Social Policy", (1998) *European Law Review*, 20–35; L. Betten, n. 41 above, at 239–260; E. Franssen, n. 3 above, at 83–91, 192–199; E. Franssen and A.T.J.M. Jacobs, "The question of representativity in the European Social Dialogue", *C.M.L.R.*, 1998, 1295–1312; M.A. Moreau, "Sur la représentativité des partenaires sociaux européens", (1999) *Droit Social*, 53–63; L. Peltzer, "Dialogue social communautaire et représentativité des partenaires sociaux", (1999) *Soc. Kron.*, 209–211; M. Schmidt, "Representativity – A Claim Not Satisfied: The Social Partners' Role in the EC Law-Making Procedure for Social Policy", (1999) *IJCLIR*, 259–267.

[43] European Court on Human Rights, *Affaire Syndicat National de la police belge*, 11 April 1975, *Série A*, nr. 19.

[44] COM (93) 600 final; Com (98) 322; COM (2002) 341 final.

of sectorial or cross-sectorial trade unions at the Community level. It also states that the affiliated organizations are themselves recognized as representative partners at Member State level and have the *capacity to negotiate agreements.*Furthermore, the Commission requires adequate structures to ensure effective participation in the consultation process.

As far as the *criteria* on representativeness required for the *negotiation* and the *conclusion* of European collective agreements *to be implemented* by a Council decision are concerned, the Commission only required that those involved in the *negotiation have a genuine interest in the matter and can demonstrate significant representation* in the domain concerned. The meaning of the concept of representation is unclear. Criteria for effective control are lacking.

32. The Court of First Instance in the UEAPME tried to elucidate the meaning of the concept of 'sufficient' representativeness required in order to implement a European collective agreement. *The analysis of the Court of First Instance* raises many questions. The objections of the Court against a transposition of European collective agreements by partners not deemed to be *sufficiently* representative, were based entirely on an *institutional* and *public* law approach of the European collective agreement as a substitute for proper legislative procedures. Considerations relating to the freedom of association were absent.

The examination of sufficient representation was not treated in a quantitative way. The Court did not verify whether the percentage of the workforce covered was effectively representative. The approach was more of qualitative nature, taking into account the nature of the interests at stake, e.g. the categories of workers covered.[45]

Neither the Commission nor the Court provided any explanation regarding by which *criteria* representativeness should be judged. The 1993 memorandum gives the impression that representativeness is defined in an *indirect* way, i.e. through representativeness of the affiliated organization at Member State level. It is always tempting to construe representativeness in a political and formal democratic way, thus counting the members of the trade unions in proportion to the total amount of employees concerned.

Such an approach can be criticized. In its 1993 *memorandum* the Commission attaches a lot of importance to the capacity to negotiate (of the confederations of Member State trade unions), to the notion of adequate structures. Those criteria might be construed as giving proof of a *qualitative* approach.

---

[45] See A. Moreau, n. 42 above, at 58 and B. Bercusson, n. 42 above, at 159.

33. The fact that representative trade unions at Community level or their affiliated organizations at national level do not unionise a majority of the workers concerned should not be construed as an obstacle to valid collective agreements.[46] The UEAPME case allows the notion of sufficient representativeness to be understood in a comparative way. In this respect it would be sufficient that the ECA is concluded by a group of trade unions which represent a majority of the *unionized* workers.

If judged otherwise, the Member States would have to develop a system of collective bargaining at the Community level, which could never be brought into effect.

The UEAPME case showed that the Court stressed that collective bargaining is basically a *voluntary* process. Representative organizations can attack directives concluded by a group of organizations not considered to be *sufficiently* representative.

There does not appears to be a standing for these organizations to be integrated through court decision in a process of collective bargaining, let alone to enforce a right to conclude to sign an existing European collective agreement or to adhere to it.[47]

34. *A contrario* the lack of representativeness might not pose any constitutional or institutional problem if ECAs were to be implemented by the procedures and practices specific to management and labour and the Member States. Furthermore, if an untransposed ECA can be recognized as having some private law binding, the question of representativeness does not seem to be pertinent either.[48] Representativeness is at stake when collective agreements are given a binding nature that exceeds the scope *ratione personae* of signatory parties and their members.

35. Representation should therefore not be construed in the ordinary *private law* meaning of the term. All trade unions are representative of the members they represent. Representation in a *neo-corporatist* vision refers to the representation of an entire collectivity of workers, and even of a

---

[46] See E. FRANSSEN, n. 3 above, at 197–199.

[47] Such a right to be integrated within the bargaining process was considered to be at odds with the latter's voluntary or spontaneous character.

Even in the Netherlands, where representative trade unions managed to be integrated through summary proceedings within the bargaining process, a right to conclude was never recognized. The problem was studied in our P.h.D. Thesis: F. DORSSEMONT, *Rechtspositie en Syndicale Actievrijheid van representatieve werknemersorganisaties*, Brugge, Die Keure, 2002, nrs. 280–287.

[48] See A. JACOBS, "From the Belgian National Labour Council to the European Social Dialogue", in C. ENGELS and M. WEISS, n. 41 above, at 326.

mythical and ideological construction of the interest of the enterprise, the profession, the economy or the general interest as such.

The approach of the Court of First Instance to compare the 'representativeness' of social partners with parliamentary or democratic representativeness is not entirely convincing. From an industrial relations point of view, 'representativeness' cannot be dissociated from the ability to threaten and/or to safeguard social peace. The simple fact of representing a vast quantity of workers is simply an indication of that more far-reaching criterion.

36. It is obvious that the selection of social partners to be consulted or to be recognized as representative is not based on objective and pre-established criteria. The question arises whether this situation is in conformity with ILO Standards.

In its case law the Committee on the Freedom of Association has insisted that the determination of representativeness should be made on the basis of objective and pre-established criteria. Although the legal articulation of these principles or guidelines is not perfectly clear, the case law seems to be inspired by a wish to safeguard the freedom of the individual *not* to join a trade union. The fact that workers might be inclined or stimulated to a join trade union, which, by chance, is effectively able to promote their interests in an efficient manner, is considered to justify a suspicion of forced membership. Furthermore, granting privileges to representatives would impede the creation of new or alternative trade unions.

The case law of the CFA has not been codified in any convention regarding the freedom of association or the freedom of collective bargaining. It has found support, however, in ILO recommendation R 163 (1981).[49]

The question arises to what extent the recognition of the highly *institutionalized* and *quasi-legislative* functions of ECAs does not undermine the *rationale* of objective and pre-established criteria. If European collective agreements *cannot* be construed as an expression of collective autonomy, thus being reduced to a public law regulatory technique, neither the freedom of association nor the right to collective bargaining seem to be at stake.

---

[49] R 163 Collective Bargaining Recommendation, 1981: '3. As appropriate and necessary, measures adapted to national conditions should be taken so that –

(a) representative employers 'and workers' organizations are recognized for the purposes of collective bargaining;
(b) in countries in which the competent authorities apply procedures for recognition with a view to determining the organizations to be granted the right to bargain collectively, such determination is based on pre-established and objective criteria with regard to the organizations' representative character, established in consultation with representative employers' and workers' organizations.'

Furthermore, the ILO standards are strictly speaking irrelevant, as the European Community is not a signatory to these instruments.

37. The analysis by the Court of the representativeness of signatory parties as a sufficient guarantee of democratic participation implies that there is no pressing need to reinforce the role of the European Parliament in the implementation procedure of the ECA.[50] Democracy is sufficiently served by involving representatives of workers and employers in elaborate rules being made applicable to workers and employers. Furthermore, a reinforcement of the role of the European Parliament tends to increase the risk of a conflict between two modes of expression of 'the will of the people'. It is at odds with the principle of horizontal subsidiarity.

§ 2. The Obligatory Peace Obligation

38. Collective agreements constitute a historic 'deal' between management and labour. Whereas trade unions wanted to exclude social competition by standardizing wages and working conditions, 'management' wanted to guarantee that the *consensus* on wages, let alone the foundations of capitalist economies, were not contested. Social Peace was management's major benefit.

It has become a scholarly custom to distinguish between the so-called obligatory and the normative part of collective agreements. This useful distinction was used by German scholars during the Weimar period.[51] It goes without saying that contractual freedom will enable signatory parties to commit themselves to various obligations.

Judging from the existing cross-sectorial and sectorial collective agreements which have been transposed by directives, *explicit* obligations range from rare to non-existent.

The most recurring obligation on the part of signatories is in fact atypical. It is an obligation to *review the application of the agreement*, if requested by one of the signatories. Such a clause is reminiscent of clauses in Social Policy directives urging the Commission to review its proposed directives after a fixed period of time.

39. In the absence of explicit obligations, one is bound to wonder whether ECAs imply *implicit* obligations for the signatory parties. Following

---

[50] *Contra:* L. Betten, n. 42 above, at 257–260; E. Franssen, n. 3 above, at 316–317.

[51] See above all the contribution and the influence of Hugo Sinzheimer. For a analysis of the author's influence: T. Van Peijpe, "De betekenis van Sinzheimer voor de wetenschap van het arbeidsrecht", in A.J. Hoekema, *Hugo Sinzheimer, rechtshervormer, arbeidsjurist en rechtssocioloog*, Amsterdam, HIS, 1993, 32–33.

German legal doctrine, it has become customary to qualify a *duty to influence* and a *social peace obligation* as implicit obligations. The reception of this influential legal doctrine within the Member States is far from general. Occasionally, a trace can be found in Member State laws regulating the legal effects of collective bargaining.[52] The question whether collective agreements contain essential implicit obligations for the signatories is often the object of scholarly debate.

In view of the differences in the legal regimes of the Member States, it seems difficult to assume that an obligation for signatories to influence the behaviour of their members with regard to the normative provisions, let alone an obligation to maintain 'social peace', is a common feature of the laws and practices of the Member States.

40. As far as the *social peace* obligation is concerned, one might argue that the EC Treaty takes a neutral stance on the right to strike and lock out. Article 137.6 EC Treaty holds that the article shall not apply to pay, the right of association, the right to strike or the right to impose lock outs.

The objection seems to be ill founded. The question at stake is whether a social peace obligation can be deduced from a collective agreement. Article 137.6 EC Treaty only applies to directives or to transpositional directives regarding ECAs; the obligatory part can hardly be conceived to be part of that transposition.

41. Any legal construction of a purely jurisprudential or praetorian nature concerning the 'implicit' will of the signatory parties to regulate the use of the right to strike is unable to hide an Achilles' heel. These limitations on the right to collective action do not stem from the *collective autonomy* of the social partners, they rather stem from ideas which legal scholars have concerning the will of social partners. According to article 6 of the European Social Charter these limitations need to fulfil the conditions of article 31.

In its latest conclusions (XVI cycle) the European Committee on Social Rights did not hesitate to conclude that the doctrine of implicit social peace obligations is not in conformity with article 6 in conjunction with article 31 of the ESC.[53]

It goes without saying that a social peace obligation is at the heart of

---

[52] Article 8 of the Dutch Law on Collective Agreements has articulated an obligation to influence. The German *Tarifvertragsgesetz* does not contain any reference to the obligatory peace obligation, nor to the duty to influence.

[53] European Committee on Social Rights, Conclusions XVI-1, Volume 1: Conclusions - Conclusions concerning Articles 1, 5, 6, 12, 13, 16 and 19 of the Charter in respect of Germany.

collective bargaining at Member State level. It is at least part of a gentlemen's agreement. The fact remains that some Member States have been extremely reluctant to recognize this obligation as a binding obligation enforceable through State law.[54]

The question remains whether the dynamics of European collective bargaining imply such a gentlemen's agreement. In our view, it is questionable whether the European trade unions have the capacity to organize a strike or collective action of a more than demonstrative nature at Community level. It is even more questionable whether the European Labour Movement has reached a level of concentration or centralization in order to control the affiliated national trade unions. It is therefore unlikely to assume that European trade unions would have committed themselves to guarantee a social peace which they are unable either to threaten nor to maintain.

42. In a country like Belgium the distinction between the obligatory and the normative part is relevant in view of the publication. Collective agreements which have been declared to be generally binding by a Royal Decree have to be published in the Belgian Official Journal (*Moniteur belge*).[55] Since only the normative part can be declared to be generally binding, the (explicit) obligatory part is not published. The practice of the Commission to publish the *entire* text of the original collective agreement does not seem to be in conformity with the understanding of the implementation procedure as a means of extending the ECA.

§ 3. Autonomy of Social Partners

43. As far as the degree of **autonomy** of the social partners is concerned, the question arises whether the Commission and the Council are *obliged* to transpose European agreements at the Community level. The wording of article 139 EC Treaty gives the impression of imposing an obligation on the Commission and the Council, or on the social partners in co-operation with the Member State, to guarantee the implementation of the ECA.[56]

The question of on whom this obligation is primarily imposed can be

---

[54] See in this respect the clear-cut position of A. LYON-CAEN refuting the existence of a social peace obligation for French workers or their trade unions, stemming from an international collective agreement: A. LYON-CAEN, "La négociation collective dans ses dimensions internationales", (1997) *Droit Social*, 366. *Contra:* E. FRANSSEN (n. 3 above, at 126–127, 153), who is in favour of the recognition of a peace obligation.

[55] Cf. Article 30 of the Law on Belgian Collective Agreements and Joint Committees.

[56] The problem was raised by B. BERCUSSON, "Maastricht: a fundamental change in European labour law", n. 31 above, at 187–188; B. BERCUSSON, "The Dynamic of European Labour Law after Maastricht", n. 31 above, at 23–26.

answered in a pragmatic way. It will depend upon the wish of the social partners.

As far as the Council is concerned the article refers to a decision being taken with a qualified majority or unanimity, depending upon the matters being regulated. The requirement of sufficient political support within the Council is at odds with the wording, which does seem to contain an obligation.[57] This *enigma* might be resolved by compelling the Commission to submit a proposal to the Council. In this respect the monitoring should be limited to the question of whether the ECA is an ECA within the meaning of the treaty. In practice the Commission also justified its decision to submit the proposal on an assessment of the necessity or the appropriateness of doing so.[58] However, the latter seems to be at odds with the wording of article 139 EC Treaty.

44. This question is very reminiscent of the question of whether Member States extending *erga omnes* collective agreements have the ability to check the appropriateness of the extension.

45. Another *enigma* is the obligation imposed upon the social partners and Member States, if requested to transpose an ECA by the signatories or in the case of a failure of the Commission and/or of the Council to implement the ECA. A declaration attached to the ASP does not seem to impose a clear-cut obligation on the social partners and Member States to act accordingly. The wording 'procedure and practices specific to management and *labour* and the Member States' is interpreted as referring to a form of (more or less) institutionalized *collective bargaining* at Member State level. Scholars do not tend to construe the formula as implying a subsequent choice between collective bargaining and legislation in its own right.

46. Other questions regarding 'autonomy' touch upon the rights which are acquainted with the paternity of the ECA by the social partners. If Community 'decisions' are supposed to be a mere transposition of pre-existing European collective agreements, logic requires them to become deprived of their object if the ECA ceases to exist as a legal instrument.[59] The social partners are able to influence the existence of the collective agreement by prescribing a term or by a unilateral resiliation or an agreement to dissolve the agreement by *mutuus dissensus*.

Over the past decade, agreements have not been concluded for a definite period nor has a *mutuus dissensus* or a unilateral resiliation occurred.

[57] See in this respect the convincing analysis of E. FRANSSEN, n. 3 above, at 287–288.
[58] See E. FRANSSEN, n. 3 above, at 207–208.
[59] See in this respect the analysis of O. DEINERT, n. 22 above, at 449–450.

Such a case might constitute basic proof by which to assess whether the directives have an auxiliary character vis-à-vis the ECA or whether in fact the social dialogue has an auxiliary character vis-à-vis the Community legislation.[60]

Another question touches upon the ability of the Council to withdraw a directive at the request of the Commission, in spite of the fact that no request by the signatories has been formulated in this respect.

47. Recent agreements show that the social partners are very fond of their paternity, revindicating a right to give authentic interpretations of the agreements in cases where there is a legal dispute.[61] It goes without saying that the partners have exceeded their competence to negotiate concerning matters covered by the term social policy.[62] On the other hand, the fact remains that these clauses have been *annexed* to the *transpositional* Community directives. The question therefore arises whether this annex is not an integral part of the directive.

48. Other questions touch upon the ability of the Community legislator to enact legislation against the explicit will of the social partners. The question may cover various hypotheses. One can imagine that the partners might request the Commission *not* to submit a proposal, without however engaging in a process of collective bargaining themselves. Such a joined negative opinion might occur during the first as well as during the second consultation.

One can also imagine the hypothesis of a collective agreement being concluded *without* a request of the signatories to transpose it into Community law, or with the request to allow the transposition to be made according to the practices of the social partners and the Member States.

The first hypothesis seems to receive a negative answer.

Article 138 EC Treaty implicitly provides that the legislative competence of the Commission and the Council can only be delayed for a period of nine months, following the expression of social partners' wish to initiate a process of collective bargaining. In the absence of such a request, the Commission and the Council *a contrario* should be considered to maintain or regain their legislative sovereignty.

---

[60] The issue seems to prove that the debate about 'collective autonomy' at Community level as a relevant conceptual framework for the construction of ECAs is far from academic.

[61] See for example the European Collective Agreement on Parental Leave.

[62] *exceeded* M. De Vos, "De Europese CAO", (2002) *Sociaalrechtelijke Kronieken*, 30; E. Franssen, "Implementation of European Collective Agreements: Some troublesome issues", (1998) *Maastricht Journal of European and Comparative Law*, 60–61.

As far as the second hypothesis is concerned, in the absence of a request by the social partners the Commission seems unable to transpose the ECA. Construed otherwise, the wording of the request would be meaningless. However, it would be at odds with the sovereignty of the Community to deny any possibility of legal intervention in the matter arranged by the ECA.

§ 4. Decisions

49. Article 139 EC Treaty provides ECAs to be transposed by Council decisions. The word 'decision' is ambiguous. It can refer to decisions *stricto sensu* or to decisions *lato senso*, i.e. any instrument producing legal effects. According to a *communis opinio*, the notion of 'decision' is *not* to be interpreted within the narrow meaning of article 249 EC Treaty. Decisions *stricto sensu* are binding in their entirety on those to whom they are addressed. Since the implementation procedure is supposed to guarantee that ECAs have a general binding for employers and employees concerned, directives are considered to be more suitable. Furthermore, since they are only binding as to the *results* to be achieved, directives rather than regulations leave it to Member States and to social partners to adapt their contents in a flexible way.[63]

50. The commonly held idea that collective agreements cannot be extended *erga omnes* through a decision having an 'individual' rather than a normative nature is surprising. The extension *erga omnes* of collective agreements within Member States tends to take place by means of legal instruments which are qualified as 'decisions'.[64]

51. Since these decisions are *ad hoc* decisions, applicable to *one* legal instrument (the collective agreement) they can be construed as having an individual nature. The fact that the decision broadens the normative character of the collective agreement does not *per se* imply that the decision itself has a normative character. According to *Belgian law*, the government is not obliged to refer to the *Conseil d'Etat (Section legislative)* prior to the decision to extend *erga omnes* a collective agreement. Since decrees with a normative or regulatory character are subject to such a previous advice, it implies that the royal decree is deprived of a normative character. The

---

[63] *communis opinio:* C. BARNARD, n. 3 above, at 93; R. BIRK, "Vereinbarungen der Sozialpartner im Rahmen des Sozialen Dialogs und ihr Durchführung", (1997) *EuZW*, 459; E. FRANSSEN, n. 3 above, at 226–229; M. DE VOS, n. 62 above, at 30; O. DEINERT, n. 22 above, at 202–204; 446–450.

[64] 'Décisions' (France); 'Besluit' (Netherlands and Belgium); 'Entscheidung' (Germany).

situation is to be compared with a law to approve an international treaty. The law implements a treaty, but has an individual character.[65]

52. Furthermore, it can be argued that the 'decision' within the meaning of article 139 EC Treaty is an instrument *sui generis*. A clear necessity to transpose ECA through directives can be disputed. As Lo Faro[66] pointed out, the choice for such an instrument constitutes a risk for the *ne varietur* transposition of the ECA. The argument that directives enable a 'flexible' implementation of a collective agreement is in fact a counterargument. A transposition by way of a *regulation* seems to offer more guarantees in order to safeguard collective autonomy.[67]

Section IV. Perspectives

53. Collective agreements tend to be qualified as complicated legal monsters. Legal disputes arising out of the interpretation, the binding effect and enforcement of collective agreements can only be solved through *effective* collective action in the spontaneous order,[68] or by a complicated legal framework regarding institutionalized collective bargaining.[69] A *lex specialis* was needed to enable collective bargaining to meet its objectives and to fulfil its functions. The *lex generalis*, the civil law, proved to be unsatisfactory to guarantee a sufficient binding effect *erga omnes* and enforcement of the instrument. In many countries it took several decades before a satisfactory solution was found for a proper legal construction of the collective agreement.

It is doubtful whether effective collective action at the Community level will take place, thus forcing employers to *respect* the content of European collective agreements.

---

[65] See in this respect P. Popelier, "Het individueel dan wel verordenend karakter van het K.B. tot algemeen verbindend verklaring van de c.a.o.'s", and "Het advies van de Raad van State, Afdeling Wetgeving", in P. Popelier, "Algemeen verbindend verklaring van de C.A.O.'s", in M. Rigaux e.a. *C.A.O.-recht*, Antwerpen, Kluwer rechtswetenschappen.

[66] A. Lo Faro, n. 22 above, at 116–121.

[67] See in this respect, the observations of R. Birk, *l.c.*, 459.

[68] A. Jacobs, n. 48 above, at 325: A. Jacobs recalls that enforcement through industrial action was the historical and natural way of enforcement within a spontaneous order, without any state intervention. The author admits that this procedure is unable to guarantee an equal and pan-European application of the standards convened upon in the ECA.

[69] Cf. Edith Franssen's pleadings for a European collective labour legislation: E. Franssen, n. 3 above, at 304–305, 318. The author pleads for a Framework-Regulation (Cf. Thesis nr. 4, annexed to the P.h.D. Thesis).

For the time being a satisfactory legal framework regulating the legal niceties of the European collective agreement is completely lacking. It would be an unwise and an extremely slow process to leave the matter up to the European courts to decide.

Obviously, a question that arises is what the functions European collective agreements are aimed at?If it is about *standardizing* some working conditions, except wage remuneration, and if *collective autonomy* is at all at stake, an appropriate legal instrument covering the binding and enforcement of the instrument seems vital. It is more than doubtful that such a framework can be elaborated by amending the EC Treaty.

Such a comprehensive legal framework needs to be elaborated in close dialogue with the European trade unions and the European employers' organizations. A historic consensus between both parties was at the basis of the drafting of the Agreement on Social Policy. It would be unwise to alter the relevant articles of the EC Treaty or to elaborate them in a framework instrument without the support of the social partners.

54. In order for the European collective agreement to be a credible expression of collective autonomy, a clear-cut recognition of fundamental workers' rights within the EC Treaty or a future Constitution is paramount. Such recognition will facilitate a balanced approach to societal problems, which are too complicated and too important to be scrutinized solely from the point of view of mere legal principles of the actual economic order.

55. The obligation of the Community to promote social dialogue (under article 137) justifies the establishment of a *voluntary* European machinery for conciliation, mediation and arbitration.[70] This objective was also expressed by the European Commissioner Diamantopoulou[71] in a speech delivered at the Conference 'Espace Judiciaire et Social Européen'. The Conference took place on 6 November 2001 and was organized by the Belgian Presidency of the European Union.

The Commissioner stated that three phenomena contributed to the necessity of such a machinery. Besides disputes arising out of the functioning of European Works Councils and the European Company, the restructuring of enterprises and the European Social Dialogue were also mentioned.

The Commission established a 'High Level Group on Industrial Relations', which made recommendations for setting up a voluntary system

---

[70] See the analysis of E. Franssen, n. 3 above, at 162–169.

[71] A. Diamontopoulo, "Solving labour disputes at a European level: possible, desirable, feasible?". For a link to the full text of the speech, see the website of the European industrial relations observatory: http://www.eiro.eurofound.ie. (Cf. Eu level developments – 25 June 2002.)

of conciliation and mediation. The 'Report of The High Level Group on Industrial Relations and Change in The European Union' was published in March 2002.[72] It represents an overview of conciliation, mediation and arbitration arrangements in the Member States. At present, a Commission document regarding the architecture of a voluntary machinery of conciliation, mediation and arbitration at Community level still has to be finalized and be the object of further consultation with the social partners.

[72] See for a link to this document the address of the website indicated in the previous footnote. The chairman of the High Level Group, Professor Fernando Valdés-Dal-Ré, has written a 'Synthesis Report on Conciliation, Mediation and Arbitration in the European Countries' (March 2002).

Chapter Two
Self-Executing Collective Agreements in EC Law*

Olaf Deinert

Introduction

1. According to Article 139 Section 1 of the Treaty Establishing the European Community (TEC) the Social Partners on Community level are allowed to build up contractual relations, including the conclusion of agreements. In terms of the implementation of such agreements two scenarios are foreseen in Article 139 Section 2 TEC. First it is possible that the Council makes a decision following a joint request of the Social Partners and a proposal of the Commission. The other scenario follows the procedures and practices specific to management and labour and the Member States. The implementation via Council decision has been chosen several times in the past (see namely directives on parental leave,[1] part-time[2] and fixed-term contracts[3]). For this reason less attention has been paid to the other method of implementation. But this could change after the Social Partners decided on this way of implementation in their latest framework agreement on telework from 16 July 2002.[4] In many cases legal scholars state – often with little or no argumentation – that this method of implementation includes the need for further transmission steps in the Member States, either by collective agreements or by legislation.[5] In my opinion I doubt whether this is true.

---

* Will be cited abbreviated: ELL-[author]: R. Blanpain (ed.), *International Encyclopaedia for Labour Law and Industrial Relations* (Kluwer Law International, The Hague).

[1] Directive 96/34/EC.

[2] Directive 97/81/EC.

[3] Directive 99/70/EC.

[4] Published on the internet: www.etuc.org/en/DOSSIERS/COLBARGAIN/telework.pdf.

[5] See e.g. A. Lo Faro, *Regulating Social Europe, Reality and Myth of Collective Bargaining in the EC Legal Order*, Hart Publishing, Oxford – Portland Oregon (2000), pp. 66–67; R. Kowanz, *Europäische Kollektivvertragsordnung* (Nomos Verlagsgesellschaft, Baden-Baden, 1999), pp. 121–125; M. Schmidt, *Das Arbeitsrecht der*

SECTION I. IS THE CONCLUSION OF AGREEMENTS NEGOTIATION OF CONTRACTS OR LEGISLATION?

2. In the legal discussion concerning the method of implementation via Council decision, the question of representativeness of Social Partners as compensation for the lack of participation of the European Parliament as a democratic element plays an important role.[6] This shows that jurisdiction and scholars regard the activities of Social Partners as some kind of 'negotiation of laws'. Although most scholars speak of European collective bargaining the truth is that they almost consider Social Partners to be making laws – albeit not alone – and not bargaining on collective agreements. This is highlighted in the famous words of *Brian Bercusson* when he called Social Dialogue 'bargaining in the shadow of the law'.[7]

3. My view on this question is a little different. First of all the Social Partners are the actors who conclude an agreement. This is the classical result of collective bargaining.[8] We characterize this result as a collective agreement, an agreement in which the actors of labour relations in organizations lay down the conditions of dependent labour. It is true that the regulation of working conditions is to a certain degree legislation for those affected – irrespective of the degree of liability. Even if collective agreements in England are 'binding in honour only',[9] they build up an external regime of rules for the individual parties of the labour contract, though they are

---

Europäischen Gemeinschaft (Nomos Verlagsgesellschaft, Baden-Baden 2001), V para. 6 with further references; G. GUÉRY, "European Collective Bargaining and the Maastricht Treaty" (1992) 131 *Int. Labour Rev.* 588; G. LYON-CAEN, "Le droit social de la Communauté Européenne après la traité de Maastricht" (1993) *Recueil Dalloz Sirey* 152; S. SCIARRA, "Collective Agreements in the Hierarchy of European Community Sources", in P. DAVIES, A. LYON-CAEN, S. SCIARRA and S. SIMITIS (eds), *European Community Labour Law: Principles and Perspectives, Liber Amicorum Lord Wedderburn of Charlton*, (Oxford, 1996), p. 202; T. TREU, "European Collective Bargaining Levels and the Competences of the Social Partners", in *liber amicorum Lord Wedderburn of Charlton*, pp. 173–174; B. TEYSSIÉ, "La négociation collective et la norme communautaire après l'entrée en viguer de l'accord européen sur la politique sociale" (1994) *La Semaine Juridique, Éd. E* 220.

[6] See e.g. CFI, decision of 17 June 1998, Case T-135/96, (1998) ECR II-2335, paras 88–94–*UEAPME/Rat*; D. GADBIN, "L'association des partenaires économiques et sociaux organisés aux procédures de décision en droit communautaire" (2000) 36 *Revue Trimestrielle de Droit Européenne* 41–47; E. FRANSSEN/A. JACOBS, "The Question of Representativity in the European Social Dialogue" (1998) 35 *CMLRev.* 1295–1312.

[7] B. BERCUSSON, "Maastricht: A Fundamental Change in European Labour Law" (1992) *Industrial Relations Journal* 185.

[8] Cf. A. LO FARO (n. 5 above), pp. 57–64, 65.

[9] The reason lies in section 179 of the Trade Unions and Labour Relations (Consolidation) Act 1992.

not obliged to use it. Nevertheless, this is only legislation in terms of effect. There are great differences between self-regulation of the affected and the formal legislation of States' actors. Here the actors are not legitimated democratically and the process in which the results are found is also fundamentally different.

4. Therefore, we can only speak about participation of Social Partners in EC legislation if the legal rule concluded is in force specifically because a State's authority has declared this after an autonomous decision. This shows in the first instance that in the method of implementation involving Council decision, the Social Partners are not able to decide alone what shall be law. On the contrary, they depend on a decision of the Council. And on the other hand the legislative authorities do not depend on the Social Partners. Although the Social Partners can push the Commission out of her initiative role for a certain time according to Article 138 Section 4 TEC, in effect they cannot prevent a legal rule they do not want, as they cannot force Council and Commission to implement a concluded agreement via Council decision. Maybe Council and Commission were well advised not to reject Social Partners' joint requests – they are not obliged to do this.[10]

5. In my opinion this leads to the following result. The Social Partners are involved in Community legislation via the process according to Article 138 Sections 2–4 TEC. But the Community authorities will ultimately take the legislative decisions. Social Partners only have the ability to make proposals and to criticize. They work as experts who give advice to the legislator founded on their special competences that result from a closer connection with the problems of management and labour.[11] Therefore, a collective agreement negotiated by the Social Partners has for the Community legislator the effect of some kind of example or recommendation. The legislator can take it and give it certain effects. But collective bargaining will not become a law-making process in this way; it will remain collective self-regulation. We know this from the Member States – with no different results. Parliaments in the Member States often adopt legal rules which have been concluded between Social Partners. They give them legal effects as laws, often with a wider scope, maybe by declaration as binding *erga omnes*, maybe by enlargement (élargissement), maybe also by fixing labour conditions via statutes which have formerly been laid down in collective agreements.

6. Result of these reflections: Social Partner agreements are, if the implementation via Council decision is chosen, only legislation in terms of their

---

[10] See e.g. B. Teyssié (n. 5 above), 221.

[11] See also for the aspect of 'legitimacy' arising from this fact: A. Lo Faro (n. 5 above), pp. 138–145.

social result; and from a fundamentally, formal point of view, they are collective agreements.[12]

Section II. Equivalence of the Ways of Implementation of Social Dialogue Agreements

7. Taking this into account for the other method of implementation, which is Community legislation to an even lesser extent because of the absence of EC authorities, we can conclude the following:

8. The Treaty regards both ways of implementation as alternatives. Therefore a third way does not exist. Therefore, the method of implementation according to the procedures and practices specific to management and labour and the Member States must always be chosen if implementation via Council decision is not possible, e.g. because the Council rejects a decision or the Commission does not propose such a decision.

9. On the other hand, this variant must be more than a pure matter of course. Imagine if there did not exist any rule in the Treaty concerning the implementation of Social Partner agreements – two principles of contract law are common to all European legal orders: a contracting party can (following the principle *pacta sunt servanda*) claim for performance with respect to the obligation the other party has promised.[13] And according to the principle that no third parties can be bound by a contract it is clear that the Members of the contracting organizations will not be bound by the agreement unless they have not given authority to contract with effects for and against them.[14,15] There would not have been need to regulate such effects of a European collective agreement that arise from the common European principles of law. The method of implementation which is discussed here must therefore give effects to collective agreements different from those that are a matter of course. Furthermore, this also follows from the fact that such effects are simply the effects of 'contractual relations'.[16] 'Agreements' in

---

[12] Explicitly contradicts A. Lo Faro (n. 5 above), pp. 132–138.

[13] See O. Lando and H. Beale (eds), *The Principles of European Contract Law, Parts I and II, Combined and revised* (2000), Art. 9–101–9–102.

[14] See for this principle of European contract law H. Kötz, *Europäisches Vertragsrecht* I, (J.C.B. Mohr, Tübingen, 1996), pp. 329–332.

[15] Cf. A. Ojeda-Avilés, "Sind Europäische Tarifverträge 'bloße Empfehlungen'?", in T. Klebe, P. Wedde and M. Wolmerath (eds), *Recht und soziale Arbeitswelt, Festschrift für Wolfgang Däubler zum 60. Geburtstag* (Bund-Verlag, Frankfurt/Main, 1999), pp. 527–531.

[16] R. Kowanz (n. 5 above), pp. 111–113. See for another point of view: T. Gilles, *Das Zustandekommen und die Durchführung von Sozialpartnervereinbarungen im Rahmen des europäischen Sozialen Dialogs* (Verlag Peter Lang, Frankfurt/M. 1999), pp. 150–160:

the sense of the Treaty must be something special compared with 'contractual relations', otherwise they would not have been mentioned expressly.

10. Starting at the point that agreements are binding only to the Social Partners and not to their members, the Social Partners were forced to use the specific national instruments to bind the parties of the individual labour contracts if they wanted to bind their members, too. Therefore they were forced to oblige their member organizations to transpose the contents of the Social Partners' agreements into collective agreements of national law which would lead to the result that the individual labour contract parties were bound at least in practice to the ECA via transposition agreements.

11. These would be the effects of agreements in the sense of Article 139 TEC – *nota bene* – if this article did not include any rule concerning the implementation of agreements. If most scholars require the first variant of implementation for transposing agreements they essentially declare that the High contracting Parties have concluded a superfluous rule in Article 139 Section 2 TEC because without this Treaty stipulation the same rule was valid.[17] But a reason why the Member States should have concluded a superfluous Treaty Section is never given.

12. In my opinion such a reason cannot be given. On the contrary, the genesis of the Treaty articles on Social Dialogue shows that the architects of the Treaty wanted to give the Social Partners an effective collective bargaining system.[18] In this way the freedom to negotiate collectively that is guaranteed in Community Law will become law in action while the bargaining system includes two alternatives with respect to bargaining systems well known in the Member States: the corporatist system and the autonomous system.

Section III. Corporatist and Autonomous Collective Agreements Systems

13. The regulation of working conditions via collective agreements is common to all labour law systems of the Member States. Nevertheless, the legal orders of collective agreements differ from country to country.

According to him contractual relations may only concern the internal connection between Social Partners and not relations to member organizations.

[17] This is also the starting point of debate in the report of Marc De Vos in this contribution.

[18] See O. Deinert, *Der europäische Kollektivvertrag* (Nomos Verlagsgesellschaft, Baden-Baden, 1999), pp. 456–458.

Corporatist systems, such as the Belgian or the Dutch systems, differ from systems with little or no State involvement as in England or Germany. Let's take a look at the implementation via Council decision. We can recognize without difficulty the corporatist system, if not in detail but in principle. This leads to the idea that the architects of the Treaty rules for implementation of Social Partners' agreements were aware of the differences of the legal systems and wanted to take care of this fact.[19] In this way the Social Partners at Community level, whose members and representatives are virtually bound to different legal systems with respect to collective agreements, can vote freely for negotiations in a corporatist manner or for bargaining in autonomy in the broadest sense of the words.

14. One could suggest that this does not reveal very much about the effects of ECA that are implemented in accordance with the procedures and practices specific to management and labour and the Member States. However, I think the opposite is true. First of all, we have two ways of implementation. So we could suggest that both variants must be more or less of the same effectiveness with respect to the effects of collective agreements, since nothing indicates that the corporatist system is privileged.

15. Furthermore, the conclusion of collective agreements is the actualization of the freedom to bargain collectively and of collective activity.[20] The freedom to bargain collectively is an aspect of the freedom of association and is a fundamental principle guaranteed as a human right in Community law. To allow Social Partners to conclude collective agreements on the one hand but to leave those agreements without any effects for the individual labour contract parties on the other hand would infringe this fundamental right. The way via Council decision does not satisfy because it leaves the Social Partners under the censorship of the Commission and of the Council.

Section IV. The Freedom to Bargain Collectively – A Fundamental Right in Community Law

16. There exist only a few indications in Community law with regard to the existence and scope of a fundamental right to bargain collectively.[21]

---

[19] See A. Jacobs, "From the Belgian National Labour Council to the European Social Dialogue", in: M. Weiss and C. Engels (eds), *Labour Law and Industrial Relations at the Turn of the Century, liber amicorum in Honour of Roger Blanpain* (Kluwer Law International, The Hague pp. , 1998), pp. 305–328.

[20] Cf. A. Lo Faro (n. 5 above), pp. 74–79, 97–103. But Lo Faro's researches start from a theoretical point of view on freedom of association and collective autonomy and not from the fundamental rights as laid down in Community law.

[21] With respect to freedom to organize see ECJ, decision of 15 December 1995, Case C-415/93, (1995) ECR I-4921 – *Bosman.*

17. Article 6 of the EU Treaty includes an admission of the fundamental rights as recognized earlier by the European Court of Justice, and furthermore, Article 136 refers to the European Social Charter (ESC) and to the Community Charter of Social Rights.[22]

18. In the meantime many judgements have been made with regard to fundamental rights. But the freedom to bargain collectively has not yet been recognized explicitly. In the *Albany* case the ECJ protected it in practice[23] by excluding it from the scope of Article 85 TEC. But the Court did not vote explicitly for the recognition of the freedom to bargain collectively and its character as a fundamental right.[24] And Advocate General JACOBS on the contrary pleaded in the *Albany* case that the freedom to bargain collectively was not covered by the freedom to organize but only by the freedom of contract.[25]

However, in my opinion the existence of this fundamental right cannot be ignored,[26] as is demonstrated by the following considerations.

19. The European Fundamental Rights Charter includes the first clue. Although it is not part of Community law in the sense of law of the Treaties or of derivative law, it has a function as symbol of high importance. Moreover it facilitates recourse to the common constitutional traditions as referred to in Article 6 Section 2 EU insofar as it reflects the consensus of the Member States' legal orders.[27] Article 12 of this Charter guarantees the freedom to organize, and Article 28 the freedom to act collectively, namely

---

[22] Treaties and Constitutions referred to hereafter are collected e.g. in: S. CLAUWAERT, *Fundamental Social Rights in the European Union, Comparative Tables and Documents* (European Trade Union Institute, Brussels, 1998).

[23] ECJ, decision of 21 September 1999, Case 67/96, (1999) ECR I-5751 – *Albany*.

[24] According to T. Blanke, Annotation to the *Albany* judgment (2000) 48 *Arbeit und Recht* 30, the Court pleaded implicitly for this freedom as a fundamental right because according to the judgment it was a barrier to the freedom of competition and therefore on the same level with it.

[25] Advocate General F. JACOBS (1999) ECR I-5751, paras 135–163 – Albany.

[26] See also B. BERCUSSON, "Freedom of Association and Fundamental Trade Union Rights", in: European Trade Union Institute (ed.), *A Legal Framework for European Industrial Relations* (European Trade Union Institute, Brussels, 1999), pp. 10–16; W. DÄUBLER, "Die Koalitionsfreiheit im EG-Recht", in U. ISENHARDT and U. PREIS (eds), *Arbeitsrecht und Sozialpartnerschaft, Festschrift für Peter Hanau* (Verlag Otto Schmidt, Köln, 1999), pp. 495–496; cf. e.g.: A. LO FARO (n. 5 above), pp. 74–89, 97–103; H. SCHMIDT, *Aufgaben und Befugnisse der Sozialpartner im Europäischen Arbeitsrecht und die Europäisierung der Arbeitsbeziehungen* (Verlag Peter Lang, Frankfurt/M. pp. 2002), pp. 165–168.

[27] See B. HEPPLE, "The EU Charter of Fundamental Rights" (2001) 30 *Industrial Law Journal* 231; K. LENAERTS and E. DE SMIJTER, "A 'Bill of Rights' for the European Union" (2001) 38 *CMLRev.* 298–299; W. DÄUBLER, "EU-Grundrechte-Charta und kollektives Arbeitsrecht" (2001) 49 *Arbeit und Recht* 382; W. DÄUBLER, "La Carta de los Derechos

with regard to negotiation and conclusion of collective agreements. This right exists according to Community law and to the legal rules and practices of the Member States. Here again we find reference to practice and legislation in the Member States, although it does not become any clearer what this means.[28] The implications of Article 28 of the Charter for the freedom to bargain collectively remain unclear.

20. In the law of nations[29] Article 11 of the EHRC guarantees the freedom to organize. It is true that the ECHR has not yet held that a right to bargain collectively is laid down in this provision.[30] On the other hand, the ESC not only guarantees the freedom to organize in Article 5, it also includes in Article 6 the freedom to conclude collective agreements, as in Section 2 of this provision the contracting States are obliged to work out procedures to facilitate the negotiation of collective agreements.

21. In the framework of the International Labour Organization the freedom to organize is guaranteed, namely through the conventions n° 87 and n° 98, which have both been ratified by all Member States. Article 4 of the convention n° 98 obliges States to work out procedures for the conclusion of collective agreements, which includes, according to the opinion of the Committee of Experts, foundation of the principle of freedom to bargain collectively.[31]

22. Furthermore, the freedom to organize is guaranteed in two United Nations Covenants which are ratified by all Member States. Those are Article 22 of the International Covenant on Civil and Political Rights and Article 8 of the International Covenant of Economic, Social and Cultural Rights. Nevertheless, more concrete provisions with regard to the contents and scope of the right are absent.

23. N° 11 of the Community Charter of Social Rights recognizes the freedom to organize, while n° 12 of the said Charter guarantees the freedom

---

Fundamentales de la Union Europea y el Derecho Colectivo del Trabajo" (2000) 17 *Revista de Derecho Social* 20; Unclear: CFI, decision of 20 February 201, Case T-112/98, (2001) ECR II-729, para. 76 – Mannesmann-Röhrenwerke.

[28] See also S. MAGIERA, "Die Grundrechtecharta der Europäischen Union" (2000) *Die öffentliche Verwaltung* 1026; according to N. PHILIPPI, *Die Charta der Grundrechte in der Europäischen Union* (Nomos-Verlagsgesellschaft, Baden-Baden, 2002), p. 30, this reference shall produce a certain lack of obligation. First thoughts about the meaning of this sentence are given by W. DÄUBLER (n. 27 above), (2000) 22–23.

[29] For guarantees in the law of nations, namely in ILO convention n° 87, see L. SWEPSTON, "Human Rights Law and Freedom of Association: Development Through ILO Supervision" (1998) 137 *Int. Lab. Rev.* 169–194.

[30] (1976) 20 ECHR A – Swedish Engine Drivers' Union.

[31] Committee of Experts, *General Survey* (International Labour Office, Geneva, 1983), para. 303.

to bargain collectively. It is left open to what extent the Charter sets out legal obligations because the guarantees laid down in it do not go beyond the common international obligations of the Member States according to law of the nations.[32]

24. Last but not least we shall take a look at the constitutional traditions of the Member States in order to find a fundamental right to organize in Community law. From the comparison of laws it should be stressed that freedom of the workers and employers to organize is guaranteed in nearly all Member States' constitutions, explicitly or as an aspect of freedom to organize in general.[33] Only for the United Kingdom can this not be said so clearly,[34] although in English legal order the right to organize is de facto acknowledged and collective bargaining is of high importance in practice.[35]

Nevertheless, it is not easy to discover whether freedom to organize includes freedom to bargain collectively. Only the Constitutions of Greece,[36] Italy[37] and Spain[38] have explicit guarantees, and in Germany the Federal Constitutional Court (*Bundesverfassungsgericht*) has ruled the same as for the constitutional provision concerning freedom to organize.[39] For the other Member States we can state that this fundamental right is recognized at least de facto in the legal order and that collective agreements are important instruments for regulating working conditions while the legal system mostly includes rules on conclusion, effects etc. of collective

[32] In principle it is not legally binding, see D. WATSON, "Social Policy after Maastricht" (1993) 30 *CMLRev.* 483. But it can be referred to for interpretation of Community law, see B. BERCUSSON, *European Labour Law* (Butterworths, London, 1996), pp. 576–577; C. BARNARD, *EC Employment Law* (Wiley, Chichester, 1996), para. 2.21.

[33] Austria: Article 12 States' Basic Law; Belgium: Article 27 Constitution; Denmark: Art. 78 Constitution; Finland: Art. 10a Constitution; France: preamble to the Constitution of 4 October 1958 in connection with Sections 6 et seq. of the Constitution of 27 October 1946; Germany: Article 9 Section 3 Basic Law; Greece: Article 23 Constitution; Ireland: Article 40 Constitution; Italy: Articles 39, 40 Constitution; Luxembourg: Article 11 Constitution; Netherlands: Article 8 Constitution; Portugal: Articles 8, 55 et seq. Constitution; Spain: Articles 7, 22, 28, 37 Constitution; Sweden: Chapter 2, Article 1, 2, 17 Constitution.

[34] See K. WEDDERBURN OF CHARLTON, *The Worker and the Law*, (3rd ed. London, 1986), pp. 277–278.

[35] For the English law concerning freedom to organize and to bargain collectively, with a European comparison, see O. DEINERT, "Kollektive Regelungsinstrumente des englischen Arbeitsrechts im europäischen Vergleich" (1999) 30 *Zeitschrift für Arbeitsrecht* 366–379.

[36] Article 22; see also G. LEVENTIS, "Das griechische Tarifvertragsrecht und seine Perspektiven", *liber amicorum Wolfgang Däubler* (n. 15 above), pp. 576–577.

[37] Article 39.

[38] Article 37.

[39] Federal Constitutional Court, Official Cases Reports (*Bundesverfassungsgerichts-Entscheidungen, BVerfGE*) Vol. 4, p. 106; 58 BVerfGE 247; permanent jurisdiction.

agreements.[40] However this statement shall not be misinterpreted in the sense that the freedom to conclude collective agreements is, in all Member States, free of attacks from public authorities.

25. Although there exists a fundamental right of collective bargaining, the Member States' legal orders contain no more concrete statements as to what effects collective agreements must have.

26. All in all the result is ambivalent: freedom to organize and the right to conclude collective agreements are at least[41] guaranteed in Community law by references of the Treaty to the law of nations and by common international obligations of the Member States. Furthermore these fundamental rights are laid down in the Member States' constitutions or at least in national labour laws. For these reasons these rights must be recognized as fundamental rights in Community law. On the other hand this allows only very general statements. That the right to bargain collectively asks for specific effects of a collective agreement cannot be concluded from the fundamental rights doctrine. Nevertheless, one statement can be given: if collective autonomy shall not only be a right on paper, collective agreements need a minimum level of effects in individual labour relations; otherwise they could not deal with their task of regulating working conditions.[42] A collective agreement which can be ignored by the parties of a labour contract would be useless.

27. But the question arises what this minimum level of effects in individual labour relations is. In this field, opinions can differ very much. For example, under English common law the stipulations are only binding for the individual contracting parties if they have decided to incorporate them into the individual contract[43] – and the same applies under Irish law.[44] This has a long tradition, and no one seems to oppose it, although the number of

---

[40] See O. Deinert (n. 18 above), p. 427 (comparison) and pp. 293–426 (country reports).

[41] Moreover, several provisions show that the Treaty accepts implicitly the right to conclude collective agreements, see for further details O. Deinert (n. 18 above), pp. 262–270; c.f. A. Lo Faro (n. 5 above), pp. 79–80.

[42] The same follows from the principle of 'double subsidiarity' or 'horizontal subsidiarity' which is laid down in the social provisions of the Treaty; see for the principle itself: B. Bercusson (n. 7 above), 184–185; S. Sciarra (n. 5 above), p. 203; for details concerning European collective agreements: O. Deinert (n. 18 above), pp. 235–253.

[43] Judicial Committee of the Privy Council (1931) Law Reports, Appeal Cases 83 – Young/Canadian Northern Railway Company; O. Kahn-Freund, P. Davies and M. Freedland, *Kahn-Freund's Labour and the Law*, (3rd edn, London 1983), pp. 166 et seq. The proof of incorporation is facilitated by the duty to give written particulars according to Section 1 Employment Rights Act 1996.

[44] See Supreme Court (*Kenny J.*), (1977) The Irish Reports 237 – Goulding Chemicals Ltd/Bolger; C. Fennell and I. Lynch, *Labour Law in Ireland*, (Dublin 1993), p. 21.

labour contracts governed by collective agreements has decreased in recent years by all accounts. On the other hand, such a low degree of obligation would be an unacceptable idea in Germany. This is the reason why the compulsory effect of collective agreements as regulated in § 4 section 1 of the Collective Agreements Act (*Tarifvertragsgesetz*) is regarded as a requirement of the constitutional guarantee of freedom to conclude collective agreements.[45]

Section V. Parallel Status of Effect

28. At this point it becomes clear that the ideas regarding what effects of collective agreements are necessary to make agreements an appropriate source of the law regulating working conditions can differ enormously from country to country. At the same time the collective agreement is in every Member State an important and effective instrument for regulating labour conditions. What satisfies in England can be insufficient in Germany. This leads to the question of why there should exist other rules for European collective agreements as for collective agreements according to national law. When we consider different concepts for effects of collective agreements, beginning with the English incorporation solution and ending with compulsory and direct effects *erga omnes* in Spanish law,[46] it seems quite ridiculous that a European collective agreement should have strictly the same effects all over Europe. It would be much more logical if it had in each Member State the same effect as a collective agreement according to national law.[47] Following this theory a European collective agreement would have different effects in Denmark than in England and different effects in Germany than in Italy. The same agreement would have in every Member State a different status of effect. Therefore, I will call this a model of parallel status of effect.

29. The words of Article 139 Section 2 TEC suggest this interpretation. The reference to procedures and practices specific to management and labour and the Member States indicates a high respect for the diversity of legal cultures in Europe. Only at first glance does the fact that reference is

---

[45] Bundesverfassungsgericht, *Arbeitsrechtliche Praxis* § 5 TVG n° 15.

[46] Articles 83 Section 3, 87 Section 3, 3 Section 1 *Ley sobre el Estatuto de los Trabajadores.*

[47] See also A. Jacobs and A. Ojeda-Avilés, "The European Social Dialogue – Some Legal Issues" (n. 26 above) pp. 65–68; A. Ojeda-Avilés, "European Collective Bargaining: A Triumph of the Will?" (1993) 9 *IJCLLIR* 279–293; A. Ojeda-Avilés (n. 15 above) pp. 527–531; O. Deinert (n. 18 above), pp. 440–443; D. Schiek, in: W. Däubler (ed.), *Tarifvertragsgesetz*, (Nomos Verlagsgesellschaft, Baden-Baden, in preparation for 2002), Einleitung G III 4 a.

also made to procedures and practices specific to management and labour indicate a need for transposition agreements. This reference only seems unusual in terms of a legal system with detailed regulation on collective labour law, namely collective agreements, as e.g. in Belgium, Germany or France. If we turn our attention to Denmark, where no Collective Agreements Act exists and the law concerning collective agreements has been ruled by the social partners themselves ('*hovedaftalen*'),[48] this reference suddenly seems to have a very deep meaning.

30. What are the dogmatic peculiarities of this concept? European Community law is mostly interpreted autonomously and its voids should equally be filled with a European perspective.[49] Therefore the question of which organizations must be regarded as Social Partners at Community level must be answered by interpreting the Treaty. In the same way it should be possible to clear up what subjects can be regulated via European collective agreements and what subjects cannot. To cover other fields: the meaning of 'transfer of undertaking' has to be determined through the interpretation of Directive 77/187/EEC (now 2001/23/EC) only. Recourse to national law is not allowed.

31. The model of parallel status of effect is – in contrast – a case of reference to (the specific) national law. Although such references are rare in Community law they are neither unknown nor impossible. For example, if public authorities deal with Community law and if no rules exist in Community law concerning the procedure, the local authorities have to apply their national legal rules according to the ECJ's permanent jurisdiction.[50] The Court judged in the same vein with regard to the employee's right to oppose the change of employer in the case of a transfer of undertaking: the consequences follow the rules set out in national labour law.[51] If a Member State is liable for not transposing a directive or for transposing it insufficiently, the questions of compensation are covered by national law.[52] And last but not least, in the Treaty a reference to national law exists

[48] See e.g. R. Nielsen, Lærbog i arbejdsret, (6th ed., Copenhagen 1996), pp. 85, 139.

[49] See e.g. ECJ, decision of 18 January 1984, Cases 327/82, (1984) ECR 107, para. 11 – *Ekro*; ECJ, decision of 27 June 1989, Cases 48, 106 and 107/88, (1989) ECR 1963, para. 11 – *Achterberg-te Riele pp.*

[50] ECJ, decision of 21 September 1983, Cases 205–215/82, (1983) ECR 2633 – *Deutsche Milchkontor*.

[51] ECJ, decision of 16 December 1992, Cases C-132/91,C-138/91 and C-139/91, (1992) ECR I-6577 – *Katsikas*; ECJ, decision of 7 March 1996, Cases C-171/95 and C-172/94, (1996) ECR I-1253 – *Merckx*.

[52] ECJ, decision of 19 November 1991, Cases C-6/90 and C-9/90, (1991) ECR I-5357 – *Francovich pp.*; ECJ, decision of 5 March 1996, Cases C-46/93 and C-48/93, (1996) ECR I-1029 – *Brasserie du Pêcheur*.

in Article 282. According to this provision the Community has in each Member State the broadest legal capacity known there for corporate bodies.

32. This last example is of great significance for the problem discussed here: it would have also been possible to create a legal rule concerning the legal capacity of the Community that would lead to a uniform legal capacity all over the Community – ignoring all possible problems arising from that. Instead of this the architects of the Treaty chose another way that leads to the applicability of different rules in the specific Member States, but uses well-proven local concepts and allows embedding of the question of capacity of the Community in the national legal system without any problems.

Section VI. Effects of an ECA Following the Theory of Parallel Status of Effect

33. Imagine that the Social Partners in the European metal industry WEM and EMF concluded an agreement on minimum vacations at a level higher than set out in Article 7 Directive 93/104/EC and chose the way of implementation according to the first alternative of Article 139 Section 2 TEC (in my view sector organizations can be regarded as Social Partners at Community level, but this will not be discussed here[53]). What would be the effects of such an agreement on the labour relations of metal workers all over Europe?

34. According to §§ 3 Section 1, 4 Section 1 of the German Collective Agreements Act, collective agreements are valid for the members of the contracting organizations as if the agreement was a law: the labour parties cannot contract out. What is necessary is that the parties are both bound: only if employer and employee are bound is the collective agreement applicable. If so mandated by their affiliated associations, umbrella organizations can conclude collective agreements in the same way (§ 2 Section 2 of the *Tarifvertragsgesetz*). The same must be true for European collective agreements: the members of an association affiliated to WEM or EMF are bound by the collective agreement which will have effects as if it was a law, provided that the other party of the employment contract is also bound by the collective agreement.

35. The rules in Portugal[54] and Italy[55] are similar: if both sides of labour are bound via membership the stipulations of the agreement will become part of the labour contract.

---

[53] See for details with further references O. Deinert (n. 18 above), pp. 468–469.

[54] Article 7 *Decreto-Lei 519-C1/79*, Articles 12–14 *Decreto-Lei 49 408*.

[55] See ELL-T. Treu, 'Italy' (June 1998), para. 429.

36. Consequently, in these countries workers who are not members of affiliated trade unions or whose employer is not member of an affiliated employers' federation do not enjoy the advantages of the collective agreement.

37. In the Netherlands[56] and in Finland[57] the stipulations of the collective agreement become parts of the individual contracts if both contracting parties are members of the associations, but an employer is furthermore obliged to offer the working conditions promised in the collective agreement to union outsiders. The same must apply to conditions set out in European collective agreements.

38. In Spain, Greece and Belgium an applicability *erga omnes* of collective agreements is known. It is questionable whether this is also true for European collective agreements. According to Spanish law a collective agreement has those effects *erga omnes* if it is an agreement covered by the *Estatuto de los Trabajadores.*[58] Any other agreements are 'collective agreements outside the statute' which have effects only if incorporated into the individual labour contract.[59] According to the theory of parallel status of effect, a European collective agreement shall be treated as a national agreement. Therefore, it is impossible to regard it as a collective agreement outside the statute only because it has not been concluded under the special rules of the *Estatuto de los Trabajadores.*[60] But they must have a quality comparable to agreements under the statutes in order to have *erga omnes* effects. For example, this is not given if the European contracting parties fail the requirements of representativeness for Spanish territory which is necessary for getting capacity to conclude agreements under the Estatuto de los Trabajadores.[61] On the other hand a collective agreement cannot be regarded as extra-statutory for the only reason that it has not been concluded in a *comision negociadora.*

In Greece we find a similar position: a general national collective agreements as well as plant agreements have normative effects *erga omnes,* while branch agreements as well as professional agreements only have direct

---

[56] Art. 12–14 *Wet op de collectieve arbeidsovereenkomst.*

[57] §§ 4, 6 Finnish Labour Contract Act, English translation in: ILO (ed.), Legislative Series (International Labour Office, Geneva) 1970 – Fin 2.

[58] See n. 46 above.

[59] See *Tribunal Central de Trabajo,* (1984) *Aranzadi Repertorio de Sentencias del TCT* nº 4915.

[60] A. OJEDA-AVILÉS (n. 15 above) p. 533, votes for treatment as collective agreement outside the statute.

[61] Articles 87, 88 *Estatuto de los Trabajadores* with Articles 6 and 7 *Ley Orgánica de Libertad Sindical.*

and compulsory effects in the case of organization membership.[62] Therefore, a European branch collective agreement such as the one in our example will only bind the members of affiliated organizations, while an overlapping agreement would have to be treated as a general national agreement and therefore would have normative effects *erga omnes.*

Erga omnes effects according to Belgian law only arise if the agreement is concluded in a proportional organ.[63] Here the same arguments as for Spanish law apply: if the contracting parties meet the requirements of representativeness[64] for the Belgian territory the European collective agreement must be treated as concluded in a proportional organ and therefore has effects *erga omnes.*[65] But one restriction has to be stressed: if the employer is not organized the individual parties have the power to contract out.[66] If this requirement is not fulfilled the general principle applies, according to which, collective agreements are automatically and with compulsory effect incorporated into the individual labour contracts that have been concluded with employers who are members of the employers' organization.[67] In this case the European collective agreement has in Belgium an effect on outsider workers.

In Finland workers of an employer who is not member of an organization enjoy the rights (not the obligations![68]) set out in a collective agreement if the agreement signifies usual custom.[69] The same applies for a European collective agreement. In this way it can get, in practice, *erga omnes* effects in Finland.

39. A European collective agreement also has effects on outsider workers in Austria,[70] France[71] and Luxembourg.[72] In Luxembourg the construction of automatic incorporation into the labour contract has been chosen.[73]

40. In Denmark the members of the affiliated organizations are bound by the collective agreement.[74] Furthermore, the employer is also obliged to

---

[62] Article 8 of the law n° 1876/1990.

[63] Article 26 *Loi sur les conventions collectives de travail et les commissions paritaires.*

[64] Article 3 *Loi sur les conventions collectives de travail et les commissions paritaires.*

[65] My former position [O. Deinert (n. 18 above), p. 451] is given up from now.

[66] See for this ELL-R. Blanpain, 'Belgium' (July 1999), paras 607–608.

[67] Articles 11, 19, 23, 53 *Loi sur les conventions collectives de travail et les commissions paritaires.*

[68] ELL-A. Suviranta, 'Finland' (Sept. 1996), para. 81.

[69] § 17 Finnish Labour Contract Act (n. above).

[70] §§ 8, 12 *Arbeitsverfassungsgesetz.*

[71] Articles 135-1, 135-2 *Code du Travail.*

[72] Article 8 *Loi concernant les conventions collectives de travail.*

[73] Article 11 *Loi concernant les conventions collectives de travail.*

[74] See P. Jacobsen, in: *Jura Europae*, 'Dänemark/Danemark', paras 62–64; ELL P. Jacobsen and O. Hasselbalch, 'Denmark' (Sept. 1998), para. 639.

apply the agreement to outsiders, but these have no corresponding rights.[75] In Sweden[76] the legal rules are similar.[77]

41. Finally, in England and Ireland the incorporation solution as previously discussed also applies to European collective agreements.

Section VII. No Objections According to Article 139 Section 2 TEC

42. The question arises whether the results found here could be rejected referring to the declaration to Article 139 Section 2 TEC.[78] The declaration reads as follows:

> 'The High Contracting Parties declare that the first of the arrangements for application of the agreements between management and labour at Community level – referred to in Article 139(2) – will consist in developing, by collective bargaining according to the rules of each Member State, the content of the agreements, and that consequently this arrangement implies no obligation on the Member States to apply the agreements directly or to work out rules for their transposition, nor any obligation to amend national legal legislation in force to facilitate their implementation.'

Although this declaration is no Treaty provision it can be helpful for interpreting the Treaty.[79]

43. This declaration does not harm the interpretation as discussed here. It is, in terms of its first part, vaguer than the text of the Treaty itself: If we have an agreement that shall be implemented, how can we develop its contents? If we have to develop contents, there does not exist an agreement yet.

44. The second part of the declaration is well compatible with my previously stated opinion: if the reference to national laws has as a consequence that the Member States are not obliged to apply the agreements directly, this is to be understood in a sense that Member States that do not know direct effects of collective agreements are not obliged to regulate such effects for

---

[75] ELL-P. Jacobsen/O. Hasselbalch, 'Denmark' (Sept. 1998), para. 642.

[76] See §§ 26, 27 *Lag om medbestemmende i arbetslivet.*

[77] See ELL-A. Adlercreutz, 'Sweden' (1997), paras 550–555.

[78] See e.g. L. Betten, "The Role of Social Partners in the Community's Social Policy Law-Making: Participatory Democracy or Furthering the Interests of Small Elites", in: *liber amicorum Roger Blanpain* (n. 19 above), p. 249.

[79] For the legal nature of the declaration see e.g. D. Watson (n. 32 above) p. 501.

European collective agreements. All in all we can regard the declaration as a proviso not to be forced by Article 139 Section 2 to adopt further legislation under the filling of gaps in the Treaty with regard to the effects of European collective agreements.

Section VIII. Consequences for the Function of Article 139 TEC

45. Regarding the results up to now it becomes clear that the Council decision has two functions.

46. In the first place it is part of a procedure of involvement of Social Partners in Community legislation. This is extremely clear when the agreement of the Social Partners has its origin in the participation of the Social Partners in the framework of Article 138 TEC.

47. Another function of the Council decision becomes apparent if we are aware that the model of parallel status of effect does not at all catch all employees within the scope of a collective agreement. The Council decision will then enlarge the group of persons bound by the agreement. At this point I do not want to discuss the question of whether, in the scope of Article 139 TEC, the Council is allowed to adopt legislative acts other than directives.[80] If it chooses – as has always happened in the past – a directive, this will lead in practice to an enlargement of the group of affected, although formally only the Member States are bound by the directive. The reason lies in the obligation of the Member States to make the subjects of the directive obligatory for all persons covered by it. And those are generally all workers and employers in the scope of the agreement, irrespective of whether they were members of an organization or not.

48. A Council decision has the function of a generally binding declaration as it is laid down for example[81] in § 5 of the German Collective Agreements Act.[82] This can only be denied with reference to the technique of regulation and by ignoring the essential point: the effect of a legal rule in social reality.

49. On the other hand, the Council decision is not comparable with an enlargement (of the agreement's autonomously stated scope), as for example

---

[80] See for this problem e.g. B. Bercusson (n. 32 above), pp. 548–549.

[81] Comparative overview on this question is given in R. Rebhahn, "Kollektivvertragsfähigkeit und Erstreckung von Kollektivverträgen in rechtsvergleichender Sicht" (2001) *Das Recht der Arbeit* 114–116.

[82] A. Jacobs (n. 19 above), p. 318; G. Guéry (n. 5 above), 591.

foreseen in French law[83] (*élargissement*),[84] because the Community authorities have no power to modify an agreement (take it or leave it position).[85] Therefore the Council cannot enforce a working time agreement in the metal industry for seafarers. The Community authorities could reach this result only by adopting another legislative act following the model of the metal workers' agreement. But for this procedure they would have to involve the Social Partners again, according to Article 138 TEC.

Conclusion and Evaluation

50. European collective agreements can have direct effect according to the model of parallel status of effect. But *erga omnes* applicability is not given in this way. However, this is not at all disadvantageous.[86] In the Member States, too, no one takes offence at the fact that collective agreements do not cover the whole labour world. Moreover, in most Member States this fact is the rule and not the exception. And no one has yet explained why the valuation should have another result for European collective agreements.

51. If Social Partners agree in the wish to reach *erga omnes* applicability they are – as in several Member States where a generally binding declaration is foreseen – free to try and request, where possible according to Articles 139 and 137 TEC, a Council decision.

52. On the other hand the Social Partners are also free, if they regard the effects according to the model of parallel status of effect, going too far, to exclude such effects e.g. by obliging only their member organizations at national level or even by giving them recommendations only.[87] Possibly direct effects in the national legal systems can also be excluded because of

---

[83] Article L 133-12 *Code du Travail*.

[84] Comparative indications for the spread of the instrument of enlargement can be found at R. Rebhahn (n. 81 above), (2001) Das Recht der Arbeit 116–117.

[85] B. Bercusson (n. 32 above), p. 548.

[86] C.f. e.g. B. Keller, Europäische Arbeits- und Sozialpolitik, (2nd ed., Oldenbourg, München, 2001), pp. 171, 256–257. In Germany e.g. trade unions think of ways of ensuring that working conditions set out in a collective agreement are not offered to outsiders, see W. Däubler, "Tarifliche Leistungen nur für Gewerkschaftsmitglieder?" (2002) Betriebsberater, pp. 1643–1648.

[87] See in this context the joint proposal of UNICE, CEEP und ETUC for the implementation of the Social Protocol, published on the internet: European Commission, "Dialogue interprofessionel – Dialogue social – 29/10/93" <europa.eu.int/comm/employment_social/soc-dial/social/euro_agr/data/en/931029.htm>, 2 November 2002.

the nature of the subjects of an agreement, e.g. in the case of mere framework agreements.

The Social Partners have so decided in their latest agreement on telework dated from 16 July 2002.[88]

[88] See n. 4 above.

Chapter Three
Collective Labour Agreements and European Competition Law: an Inherent Contradiction?

Marc De Vos

Introduction

1. The relationship between collective labour relations and competition law has been a longstanding and intricate issue in the law of most EU Member States. It should come as no surprise then, that in the absence of specific European legislation on the topic, the European Court of Justice (hereinafter: ECJ) would eventually become entangled in it. It is only surprising that it took forty years before it was forced to do so. In the by now (in)famous cases of *Albany*, *Brentjens*, and *Drijvende Bokken* the Court was required to confront collective labour agreements with European competition law in its most emblematic shape: article 81 of the Treaty Establishing the European Community (hereinafter: TEC).

The angle of collective labour agreements determines my focus. This article explores the relationship between *EC competition law in general*, i.e. including but not limited to article 81 TEC, and *collective labour agreements* in general. For the scholar, the latter concept may require a precise preliminary definition, but that would be futile as well as useless for my purpose. A common-sense understanding as agreements that collectively settle labour conditions will suffice as a starting point and includes the European collective agreements which labour and management can conclude in the context of article 139(1) TEC.[1] Further and technical delineation relevant to our endeavour will essentially follow from the current ECJ case-law. A critical appraisal of that case-law, both in its analysis and in its potential consequences, indeed forms the core of this contribution (Sections III and IV). However, that appraisal cannot be separated from the ideological or economic background of the issue (Section I), nor can it be attempted without a general *ex ante* legal analysis that includes the previous ECJ case-law

[1] See M. De Vos, "De Europese CAO" (2002) *Sociaalrechtelijke Kronieken* 11, at 14–15.

(Section II). Our focal point throughout remains exclusively the *European dimension*, with minor comparative references to the national law of EC Member States.

Section I. The Ideological or Economic Background

§ 1. Positive and Negative Economic Effects of Collective Bargaining

2. Collective bargaining, its twin brother, unionization, and their end-product of labour agreements that collectively settle labour conditions for a given level – plant, sector, cross-industry, transnational or even European – may to some extent promote economic efficiency. Indeed, unions and collective bargaining may reduce the transaction costs related to the negotiation of individual labour contracts, deter opportunistic behaviour from both employees and employer, avoid costly strikes, warrant the fulfilment of long-term labour contracts, and even help to monitor the effectiveness of management.

Moreover, unions may be a convenient answer to the public goods problem in companies. Many features of the workplace, such as safety conditions, pollution, comfort, productivity and working speed, working hours, discipline etc. are of a public good nature: many people benefit, or no one does. The individual worker often has an insufficient incentive to provide information on these matters to management, because benefits accrue to workers collectively. Specialization may also deprive the individual worker of the necessary knowledge to make valuable assessments. Unions and the collective bargaining process can therefore serve as an informed and informative communication channel, allowing management to introduce timely improvements in production or working conditions.

These potentially beneficial effects – from an economic and efficiency perspective – of unions and collective bargaining have been suggested in theoretical and empirical studies that are both relatively recent and relatively controversial.[2] However recent and controversial, these studies have already penetrated law academia and even the World Bank.[3] Whether

[2] See R. Freeman and J. Medoff, *What Do Unions Do?*, New York, Basic Books, 1984, 8–10; B. Klein, R. Crawford and A. Alchian, "Vertical Integration, Appropriable Rents, and the Competitive Contracting Process" (1978) 21 *J. L. & Econ.* 297; R. Lande and R. Zerbe, "Reducing Union's Monopoly Power: Costs and Benefits" (1985) 28 *J. L. & Econ.* 297, at 300–302.

[3] See and comp., e.g., H. Collins, P. Davies, and R. Rideout, *Legal Regulation of the Employment Relation* (eds.), London, Kluwer Law International, 2000; S. Deakin and F. Wilkinson, "Rights vs Efficiency? The Economic Case for Transnational Labour Standards" (1994) 23 *I.L.J.* 289; World Bank, "Economies Perform Better in Coordinated Labor Markets", Press Release 2003/211/S, www.WorldBank.org,

unions in their present legal form are the only and most effective answer to the efficiency problems they are claimed to solve, remains overlooked in this unison.

3. More traditional and more documented is the opposite view, that unions and collective bargaining diminish efficiency and hinder economic development, and in the process undermine the very purpose they aim to achieve: worker protection through high employment levels. Unions and collective labour agreements, the argument goes, tend to keep wages artificially high without taking into account the resulting loss of employment. Collective labour agreements typically drive the labour price above its natural equilibrium in a free market, thus resulting in a diminishing demand for labour while artificially excluding jobs from the labour market. Jobs which no longer produce their cost are indeed shelved or transferred to a cheaper production area, and labour is increasingly replaced by capital. High labour costs, moreover, imply higher costs for products and services, with an adverse effect on their consumption, which in turn affects production and its demand for labour. This vicious circle is exacerbated if unions occupy their usual monopolistic or oligopolistic positions for the determination of labour conditions.[4]

Underlying and permeating this virulent critique of unions and collective bargaining is Austrian-school economic mantra or, to use a more common phrase, neo-liberal doctrine. Rooted in a fundamental, perhaps even fundamentalist belief in *freedom*, this doctrine hails the *free market* as the ultimate tool for societal organization, including the organization of labour conditions. It is only through free and unfettered exchange between individuals that the labour market will achieve maximum employment and other markets their maximum development to the benefit of all, including the workers themselves. Organized labour and collective bargaining per se reduce the amount of employment available, and prevent workers – especially the disadvantaged – from doing work they would otherwise wish to

---

12 February 2003. See also C. BARNARD, *EC Employment Law*, Oxford, Oxford University Press, 2000, 557.

[4] See the overview and references in R. VAN DEN BERGH and P. CAMESASCA, "Irreconcilable Principles? The Court of Justice Exempts Collective Labour Agreements from the Wrath of Antitrust" (2000) 25 *E.L.Rev.* 492, at 503–507.

For a recent empirical study that supports the assumed economic deficiency of unionism, see ALLEGHENY INSTITUTE FOR PUBLIC POLICY, *Unionism and Economic Performance: Pennsylvania and Peer States*, May 2003, available at www.allegheny institute.org.

do, and at the price of reducing the productivity of labour and thus the general level of real wages for all.[5]

§ 2. A Free (European) Labour Market?

4. We need not inquire here which of the two postulated economic effects of unionization and collective bargaining is either correct or dominant. We rather need to ascertain whether the legal order of the European Community has sided for one or the other economic theory, and how that affects the possibility for collective bargaining under EC law.

There can be no doubt that the European Community, in its economic component previously known as the European Economic Community, has pioneered a free market revolution roughly along neo-liberal or Austrian-school economic lines. The EEC was established to create a free common market, based on the free movement of labour, goods, services and capital. These four freedoms match the four elements of 'natural liberty' in Adam Smith's *Wealth of Nations*, the Old Testament for contemporary neo-liberals.[6] The founding fathers of the EEC moreover believed that a common market founded on these freedoms would in time ensure optimum economic growth, optimum employment, and the constant improvement of living and working conditions.[7] Through Adam Smith's *invisible hand*, a free and efficient market would spontaneously raise labour standards: a resounding endorsement of the classic neo-liberal market doctrine.[8]

5. EC competition law serves a variety of functions, the two most important and most commonly recognized of which are the assurance of effective free competition and the integration of the internal European market.[9] These two essential functions are not necessarily compatible, as we shall see in our critique of *Albany*. What interests us here is the role of EC competition law as a bulwark of effective free competition guaranteeing an efficient allocation of resources. In that capacity, EC competition law is the natural

---

[5] See M. Friedman, *Capitalism and Freedom*, Chicago, The University of Chicago Press, 2002, 124; F.A. Hayek, *Law, Legislation and Liberty*, III, *The Political Order of a Free People*, London, Routledge, 1998, 144.

[6] A. Smith, *An Inquiry into the Nature and Causes of the Wealth of Nations*, 1776.

[7] See M. Shanks, "The Social Policy of the European Community" (1977) *C.M.L.Rev.* 14.

[8] C. Barnard, *EC Employment Law*, n. 3 above, at 2; T. Hervey, *European Social Law and Policy*, Longman, Harlow, 1998, 7.

[9] See C. Bellamy and G. Child, *European Community Law of Competition*, London, Sweet & Maxwell, 2001, at 39–43; A. Jones and B. Sufrin, *EC Competition Law*, Oxford, Oxford University Press, 2001, at 4–17 and 27–35; R. Whish, *Competition Law*, London, Butterworths, 2001, at 15–21.

apanage of the common market. The four freedoms that form the foundation of the European common market imply four spheres of free exchange, of free competition. The question of whether, or to what extent, that free competition and its legal protection apply to the organization of labour relations and/or of the labour market, is therefore self-evident, at least today. It was not self-evident in 1957 nor for any time soon after, since both the single market and a genuine European dimension of labour and employment law proved long in the making.

Confrontation of *collective bargaining* and *collective labour agreements* with a free market and free competition logic inevitably yields conflict. Collective labour agreements on wages and other labour conditions *intrinsically* form an obstacle to free and unfettered competition on the labour market, because employees and employers respectively cannot offer or hire labour for a price below the minimum conditions. The very purpose of collective labour agreements that exceed the mere company level is precisely to *avoid competition* in labour conditions between companies,[10] at least competition to the bottom.[11] Moreover, collective labour agreements beyond the single company level resemble *cartels* to the extent that they partially control price competition by fixing the labour component of production costs, or whenever they impose rules in relation to third parties.[12] Finally, the position of unions – whether worker or employer unions – in the negotiation of collective labour agreements is often of a *monopolistic* or *oligopolistic* nature inimical to free competition and antithetical to antitrust regulation.[13]

However, for this cataract of calamities to descend upon the social partners in the collective bargaining process, *one must first and in principle agree to apply the free market and free competition paradigm to the labour dimension.* Only when labour relations and conditions are *a priori* brought under the free market realm can their organization through collective bargaining become inherently contentious through the freedom of competition requirements. That is the big 'if' that the existing literature largely ignores when it explores the interactions between competition law and collective labour law without determining whether both are indeed in the same sphere. The following section makes this necessary and preliminary

---

[10] F. Gamillscheg, *Kollektives Arbeitsrecht*, München, Beck, 1997, 692; M. Mok, "Kartel en collectieve arbeidsovereenkomst", in *Hedendaags arbeidsrecht. Liber amicorum G. Levenbach*, Smasom, Alphen aan den Rijn, 1966, 242, at 242.

[11] Collective labour agreements typically fix minium conditions.

[12] M. Mok, "Kartel en collectieve arbeidsovereenkomst", n. 10 above, at 248 and 251.

[13] *Ibid.*, at 246–247; comp. R. Van den Bergh and P. Camesasca, "Irreconcilable Principles? The Court of Justice Exempts Collective Labour Agreements from the Wrath of Antitrust", n. 4 above, at 502.

inquiry by identifying principled legal obstacles to the inclusion of labour relations in the free competition prism and confronts them with the ECJ's case-law prior to the *Albany* watershed.

Section II. Labour, Free Market, and Free Competition: One Sphere?

§ 1. Traditional Legal Obstacles to a Modern Trend

6. If free market and free competition are indeed to be its residual and natural habitat, the law of (collective) labour relations needs to break away from its historical origins. In continental Europe, the legal organization of labour relations is to a large extent the product of an early 20th-century reaction against 19th-century exploitation of workers by an all-powerful management. Balancing the power within the employment relationship (protection of the worker) and within the company (works councils, unions, strikes, ...), is the cornerstone of that reaction. Consequently, traditional labour legislation rests on two basic premises: first, *dependence* of the exploited, endangered and subordinate worker; second, a *collective* approach to the labour force and its representation, as a means for balancing management power and ensuring the rights of each worker.

On the other hand, competition law, the free market it protects and its neo-liberal roots consider employers and employees as equals.[14] The dynamic interaction of free individuals is the context in which collective labour bargaining serves not to protect but to oppress.[15] It is therefore tempting to see the growing attention for the relationship between competition law and collective labour relations as reflecting a more individualistic approach toward labour relations. Several civil law countries have recently witnessed a renaissance of the role of the individual employment contract and of the use of (Napoleonic) general contract law in employment law issues.[16] This renewed interest for the individual agreement and for what

---

[14] R. Van den Bergh and P. Camesasca, "Irreconcilable Principles? The Court of Justice Exempts Collective Labour Agreements from the Wrath of Antitrust", n. 4 above, at 502.

[15] F.A. Hayek, *Law, Legislation and Liberty*, III, *The Political Order of a Free People*, n. 5 above, at 144.

[16] See, e.g.:

– for Belgium: M. Jamoulle, "Le contrat de travail à l'épreuve du temps" (1998) 17 *Sociaalrechtelijke Kronieken* 472;

– for France: A. Lyon-Caen, "Actualité du contrat de travail" (1988) *Droit Social* 540; P. Waquet, "Le renouveau du contrat de travail" (1999) *Revue de Jurisprudence Sociale* 383; J. Barthélémy, "Droit de la durée du travail: la tendance à la contractualisation" (2003) *Droit Social* 25;

is essentially the statutory hallmark of 19th-century liberalism indicates an underlying trend towards more individualism and emancipation in labour relations. The prominence of the competition law debate may exemplify this, together with other evolutions such as the 'on line' phenomenon, the proliferation of employment discrimination laws, the dilution of the subordination concept, the erosion of the notion of 'employer', and the expansion of financial employee participation.[17]

7. Emancipation and individualism may be the signs of the times, but the existing legal architecture of labour relations remains largely inspired by the classic labour law model, where individual liberty is subordinated to collective representation and to the societal interest of labour relations.[18] The kernel of that traditional labour and employment law is precisely *not* to abandon labour relations to free exchange and competition, but instead to correct or avoid the expected excesses of *laissez faire* liberty. Underlying the pervading law of labour relations are ideological convictions that clash heavily with the neo-liberal convictions underpinning the infusion of market and competition logic. This ideological chasm receives its most emblematic legal expression in the ILO Constitution's credo that 'labour is not a commodity',[19] a clear Marxist phraseology that diametrically opposes the neo-liberal approach of labour relations.[20] Under the 'no commodity' banner, even the concept of a labour 'market' seems *a priori* excluded, let alone the organization of labour relations on a free market and free competition platform. In the United States, the conviction that 'the labour of a human being is not a commodity or article of commerce' motivates a partial statutory exemption from antitrust laws for labour organizations.[21] Some European authors essentially make the same claim when they assert

– for the Netherlands: P.F. Van Der Heijden, "Een nieuwe rechtsorde van de arbeid. Op zoek naar een andere architectuur van het arbeidsrecht", in P.F. Van Der Heijden, R.H. Van Het Kaar and A.C.J.M. Wilthagen, *Naar een nieuwe rechtsorde van de arbeid?*, Sdu Uitgevers, 1999, 10–12.

[17] See M. De Vos, "On line rights of workers. Electronic interaction in the workplace. General reflections and some Belgian perspectives", in R. Blanpain (ed.), *The Evolving Employment Relationship and the New Economy: the Role of Labour Law & Industrial Relations*, The Hague, Kluwer Law International, 2001, 235–240.

[18] Comp. A. Weill, *Le principe de la relativité des conventions en droit privé français*, Paris, Dalloz, 1938, at 20–21.

[19] Article I, a of the Declaration of Philadelphia concerning the aims and purposes of the ILO.

[20] See L. Von Mises, *Socialism*, Liberty Fund, Indianapolis, 1981, at 391.

[21] See § 6 of the Clayton Act, 38 *Stat.* 730 (1914), now 15 *U.S.C.* § 17.

that competition law concerns only the market for products and services, and not the labour market.[22]

The distinction between labour and genuine commodities such as products and services is of course superficial and artificial. Since labour is necessary to produce the 'genuine' commodities, its organization indirectly but necessarily affects their market. This reality, combined perhaps with the limited legal force of the ILO Constitution, may explain why the Member States of the EC, notwithstanding their membership of the ILO, typically have no blanket labour exemption in their national competition law. If there is any rule to be drawn from the EC Member States, it is one of careful balancing that amounts to a partial immunity from antitrust law.[23] In any event, Member State solutions to the labour v. competition conundrum at the national level are wholly separate from the EC level where no dogmatic statement on the nature of labour obscures the debate.[24]

8. The contentious relationship between traditional labour law and modern competition law reaches its apogee with the law of collective bargaining. Under the classic labour law paradigm, collective bargaining is necessary to promote bargaining equality between labour and capital. In a free competition world, however, collective bargaining is, as we have seen, intrinsically invidious.[25] The preliminary question to address here is whether the existence of a legal framework supporting collective bargaining in the EC implicitly offers an in principle objection to the application of EC competition law. This limits our inquiry to the string of international and European sources that recognize the *freedom of association and collective bargaining*, in particular in the context of the Council of Europe and the European Community.[26]

---

[22] F. Gamillscheg, *Kollektives Arbeitsrecht*, n. 10 above, at 692; A. Lyon-Caen, "Droit social et droit de la concurrence", in *Les orientations sociales du droit contemporain. Liber amicorum Jean Savatier*, Paris, P.U.F., 1992, 331, at 331–332; comp. M. Mok, "Kartel en collectieve arbeidsovereenkomst", n. 10 above, at 245.

[23] See the comparative overview in Advocate-general F. Jacobs' opinion in *Albany*, *Brentjens*, and *Drijvende Bokken*, respectively C-67/96, joined cases C-115/97, C-116/97, C-117/97, and C-219/97, (1999) *E.C.R.* I-5751, para. 80–112; R. Van den Bergh and P. Camesasca, "Irreconcilable Principles? The Court of Justice Exempts Collective Labour Agreements from the Wrath of Antitrust", n. 4 above, at 495–499.

[24] Irrespective of any potential conflict between the national law and EC law. Our only purpose is to determine the applicable EC law.

[25] *Supra*, at para. 5. Promotion of bargaining equality was the major *ratio legis* behind the statutory exemption of labour from federal antitrust legislation in the United States: see R. Lande and R. Zerbe, "Anticonsumer Effects of Union Mergers: an Antitrust Solution" (1996) 46 *Duke Law Journal* 197, at 206–207.

[26] Art. 11 European Convention on Human Rights and Fundamental Freedoms; art. 6 European Social Charter; art. 139(1) TEC; art. 12 Community Charter of the Fundamental Social Rights of Workers; art. 28 Charter of Fundamental Rights of the European Union.

There is considerable literature on the question of whether the freedom to bargain collectively amounts to a *fundamental right*.[27] The existing case-law, both from the Court of First Instance and from the European Court of Human Rights, refuses to recognize a fundamental right that implies a duty to enter into negotiations with a given organisation.[28] Beyond the question of whether freedom of collective bargaining entails duty of collective bargaining, the debate over its status as a fundamental right seems largely semantic to our inquiry. It is generally not suggested that the status of 'fundamental right' would allow the social partners to discard community law to which they would otherwise be subjected, let alone equally fundamental principles such as the internal market and its free competition rules.[29] This is especially true in the context of the European social dialogue promoted and organized by articles 138–139 of the TEC. Many pundits agree that as a matter of course, European collective labour agreements concluded through articles 138–139 TEC should respect all relevant EC and national law.[30] In other words, the mere recognition of a fundamental right to bargain collectively would not shelter collective bargaining from the outside legal world. It therefore does not *per se* exclude the applicability of EC competition law rules.[31] In this respect, the EC cannot be distinguished from Member States where freedom of collective bargaining and free competition coexist without explicit hierarchy and with no statutory framework to resolve their apparent contradiction.[32]

The advent of the Charter of Fundamental Rights of the European Union (hereinafter: EU Charter) does not alter our conclusion. Its article 28 recognizes a genuine right to negotiate and conclude collective agreements at the appropriate levels, but that does not imply a general exemption from

[27] For an overview with a positive inclination, see O. Deinert, *Der europäische Kollektivvertrag*, Baden-Baden, Nomos, 1999, 254–435.

[28] See, *inter alia*, ECHR, *Svenska Lokmannaförbundet*, 6 February 1976, (1976) *Eur. Court H.R. Rep.*, Series A, no. 20; ECHR, *Smidt and Dahlström*, 6 February 1976, (1976) *Eur. Court H.R. Rep.*, Series A, no. 21; ECHR, *Gustafsson*, 25 April 1996, (1996) *R.J.D.*, II, no. 9; ECHR, *Wilson & National Union of Journalists*, 2 July 2002, nos. 30668/96, 30671/96 and 30678/96; CFI, 17 June 1998, *UEAPME*, T-135/96, (1998) *E.C.R.* II-2335.

[29] See and comp. S. Graf von Wallwitz, *Tarifverträge und die Wettbewerbsordnung des EG-Vertrages*, Frankfurt am Main, Peter Lang, 1997, at 79–80 and 92–106.

[30] See C. Barnard, *EC Employment Law*, n. 3 above, at 569; M. De Vos, "De Europese CAO", n. 1 above, at 16–17; E. Franssen, *Legal Aspects of the European Social Dialogue*, Antwerp, Intersentia, 2002, at 111–112; G. Lyon-Caen and A. Lyon-Caen, *Droit social international et européen*, Paris, Dalloz, 1993, at 339; comp. A. Lo Faro, *Regulating Social Europe. Reality & Myth of Collective Bargaining in the EC Legal Order*, Oxford, Hart Publishing, 2000, at 107–108.

[31] *Contra* C. Barnard, *EC Employment Law*, n. 3 above, at 569.

[32] Comp., e.g., with France: B. Edelman, "A bas le droit du travail, vive la concurrence!" (1992) *D. Chronique*, 1, at 3.

competition law rules.[33] Irrespective of the essentially political value of the EU Charter in its current shape, it only recognizes the right to collective bargaining 'in accordance with Community law and national laws and practices'. That caveat supports an inclusion rather then an exclusion of competition law. The EU Charter moreover also recognizes the freedom to conduct a business (art. 16). Like the TEC itself, the EU Charter therefore maintains the tension between free competition and free collective bargaining.[34]

9. If it cannot per se shield collective bargaining from competition law intrusion, what then is there to learn from the recognition of the freedom of collective bargaining in both the TEC and other European sources? It is fair to assume that this recognition cannot be meaningless. The unrestricted application of competition law in its unidimensional condemnation of collective bargaining as inherently odious would render it meaningless. Since the other extreme of untouchable collective bargaining is equally untenable, a middle ground will have to be found.[35] It is there that we leave abstract legal arguments and dive into the case-law of the ECJ prior to *Albany*.

§ 2. Precedents at the EC Level

10. *Albany* may have been the first case in which collective bargaining was squarely confronted with EC competition law, but it was not without its precedent on the broader issue of how employment policy and the organization of the labour market combine with the internal market, its fundamental freedoms and its free competition standards. A brief overview of cases, with no claim to exhaustiveness, clearly demonstrates a common approach that can serve as a benchmark in our evaluation of *Albany* and its progeny.

1. State Aid for Employment

11. In the context of *state aid*, the ECJ has consistently held that the social aim of state measures is not sufficient to exclude them outright from classification as aid for the purpose of article 87 of the TEC. Measures

---

[33] *Contra* E. Bribosia en O. De Schutter, "La Charte des droits fondamentaux de l'Union européenne" (2001) *Journal des Tribunaux* 281, at 292.

[34] W. Däubler, "EU Charter of Fundamental Rights and Collective Labour Law", in G. Van Limberghen and K. Salomez, *Sociale grondrechten als bakens voor een vernieuwd sociaal recht. Liber amicorum professor Maxime Stroobant*, Gent, Mys & Breesch, 2001, at 78.

[35] S. Graf von Wallwitz, *Tarifverträge und die Wettbewerbsordnung des EG-Vertrages*, n. 29 above, at 106.

which, in various shapes and sizes, are aimed at combating unemployment and/or at reducing labour cost therefore do have to pass article 87 muster, irrespective of their social aims.[36] This line of cases teaches us two things.

First, employment and employment policy objectives do not per se justify an exemption from competition law. Similarly, when the ECJ is asked whether national *employment legislation* which spares small businesses amounts to state aid, its negative answer does not follow from any labour exemption. On the contrary, the Court does apply competition rules to the employment legislation in question, but finds no advantage that can be considered 'state aid' within the meaning of article 87 TEC.[37]

Second, measures that reduce labour costs are considered to be of the same nature as outright subsidies: both mitigate the charges which are normally included in the budget of an undertaking and therefore influence its competitive position.[38] This second conclusion clearly demonstrates that no dogma of 'non-commodity nature' can separate labour from market competition under EC law. Whether labour is or is not a commodity, its organization and the resulting cost do impact competition on the commodity market.[39] The ECJ reasons in the same vein when it extends competition rules to agreements that merely uniform *terms and conditions*, not unlike collective agreements that determine labour and employment conditions.[40]

12. What is true for state aid aimed at reducing labour cost in general is equally true when that state aid is attributed in the context of *collective labour agreements*. The ECJ upheld a conviction for illegal state aid against France for granting specific financial advantages as a *quid pro quo* for undertakings which, through sectorial collective labour agreements, had reorganized and reduced working time. The aid in question was promised in framework agreements accompanying the collective labour agreements, but that did not deter the ECJ from applying its traditional state aid analysis.[41] Without squarely confronting the relationship between collective labour agreements and competition law as such, this case nonetheless

---

[36] See, e.g., ECJ 29 February 1996, *Belgium v. Commission*, C-56/93, (1996) *E.C.R.* I-723; ECJ 26 September 1996, *France v. Commission*, C-241/94, (1996) *E.C.R.* I-4551; ECJ 29 April 1999, *Spain v. Commission*, C-342/96, (1999) *E.C.R.* I-2459; ECJ 17 June 1999, *Belgium v. Commission*, C-75/97, (1999) *E.C.R.* I-3671.

[37] ECJ 30 November 1993, *Nurhan Sidal*, C-189/91, (1993) *E.C.R.* I-6185.

[38] ECJ 1 December 1998, *Ecotrade*, C-200/97, (1998) *E.C.R.* I-7907, para. 34.

[39] *Supra*, at para. 7.

[40] See C. Bellamy and G. Child, *European Community Law of Competition*, n. 9 above, at 221–223 and 260–265; A. Jones and B. Sufrin, *EC Competition Law*, n. 9 above, at 652; R. Whish, *Competition Law*, n. 9 above, at 439–441.

[41] ECJ 5 October 1999, *France v. Commission*, C-251/97, (1999) *E.C.R.* I-6639.

suggests an orthodox evaluation of measures that, through a process of collective agreements, affect competition by affecting labour costs.

The analysis of state aid for employment through the competition law prism has become so natural that the Commission has recently adopted a regulation that standardizes the conditions for a partial group exemption under article 87.3 TEC.[42] As its preamble makes clear, the regulation is based on the premise that employment costs form part of the normal operating costs of any enterprise, which in turn implies competition effects of employment aid.[43] Again no principled separation of EC competition law and the organization of employment conditions is entertained.

2. Employment Agencies and the Provision of Manpower

13. The formation of an internal European market based on free exchange and free competition has successfully liberalized the *provision of manpower through employment agencies.* Several Member States initially blocked free competition in this field through special licence requirements or public monopolies. These measures were typically justified by the particular nature of a service – employment procurement – worthy of special consideration, especially since it could be covered by EC provisions both on social policy and on free movement and free competition. The ECJ was unconvinced. The special nature of certain services cannot in principle remove them from the ambit of the rules on the *freedom to supply services.* However, the impact of the business of employment procurement on the labour market and on the labour force may justify a legitimate policy goal and measures in proportion to it.[44] Similarly, the special nature of employment procurement does not justify an in principle exemption from *competition rules.* For the ECJ, employment procurement is the activity as an intermediary between supply and demand in employment relationships, and as such a business activity within the meaning of EC competition law. However, monopolistic public placement offices escape competition law scrutiny to the extent necessary for the discharge of their duties.[45]

This line of cases adopts a common approach to an issue of labour

---

[42] Commission Regulation 2204/2002 of 12 December 2002 (*OJ L* 337, 13 December 2002, 3), in execution of Council Regulation 994/98 of 7 May 1998 (*OJ L* 142, 14 May 1998, 1).

[43] Preamble, sections 16–17.

[44] See, inter alia, ECJ 3 December 1974, *Van Binsbergen*, 33/74, (1974) *E.C.R.* 1299; ECJ 18 January 1979, *van Wesemael*, 110 and 111/78, (1979) *E.C.R.* 35; ECJ 17 December 1981, *Webb*, 279/80, (1981) *E.C.R.* 3305.

[45] See, inter alia, ECJ 30 April 1974, *Sacchi*, 155/73, (1974) *E.C.R.* 409; ECJ 23 April 1991, *Höfner*, C-41/90, (1991) *E.C.R.* I-1979; ECJ 11 December 1997, *Job Centre*, C-111/94, (1997) *E.C.R.* I-7119.

market organization versus economic freedom. First, there is no labour exemption that extracts the organization of the labour market from free market or free competition logic. Instead, the ECJ again clearly sees labour organization as just another form of economic organisation. Second, however, the implication of labour and employment justifies a balanced accommodation under the overarching free market and free competition umbrella, in respect of legitimate social policy aims.

3. Prohibition of Sunday Work

14. The balanced accommodation of employment regulation within the framework of a common market based on free exchange and free competition is also reflected in the ECJ's case law regarding *Sunday work prohibitions.* National working time provisions prohibiting the employment of workers on Sundays are subjected to the rules of the common market, including the free movement of goods, the freedom to provide services, and the prohibition for Member States to support agreements, decisions or practices which distort free competition. However, the legitimate aim of worker protection makes them compatible with those rules to the extent that their restrictive effects are not disproportionate to that aim.[46] Here again, the ECJ does not extract the organization of employment conditions from the free market and free competition sphere, but rather accommodates it within certain limits, in due respect of its legitimate aim.

4. Tourist Guides

15. National legislation protecting and organizing the activity of *tourist guides* has repeatedly clashed with the TEC's freedom to provide services provisions.[47] One case in particular reveals the attitude of the ECJ on the relationship between collective labour relations and the free internal market. A Greek law prescribed a mandatory legal form of employment relationship for tourist guides pursuing their profession in agreement with travel or tourist agencies. The said law had settled a longstanding collective labour dispute in Greece, and its necessity for maintaining industrial peace was invoked to justify any negative impact on the free movement of services. Unsurprisingly, the ECJ first subjects what is Greek employment legislation to the protection of free movement in services, once more clearly forfeiting any labour exemption from the organization of the internal market.

---

[46] See ECJ 23 November 1989, *Torfaen*, C-145/88, (1989) *E.C.R.* I-3851; ECJ 28 February 1991, *CGT*, C-312/89, (1991) *E.C.R.* I-997; ECJ 28 February 1991, *Marchandise*, C-332/89, (1991) *E.C.R.* I-1027.

[47] See, e.g., ECJ 26 February 1991, *Commission v. France*, C-154/89, (1991) *E.C.R.* I-659; ECJ 26 February 1991, *Commission v. Italy*, C-180/89, (1991) *E.C.R.* I-709.

Secondly, the Court recognizes that proportional measures justified by overriding reasons of general interest may justify a barrier to the free movement of services, but refuses to include the contested law in that category. For the ECJ, maintaining industrial peace and settling collective labour disputes are plain economic aims, not reasons of general interest.[48] A clearer inclusion of collective labour relations in the spectrum of the common economic market can hardly be imagined.

5. *Conclusion*

16. Our cursory overview of cases reveals a constant policy along two axes. First, the ECJ refuses to make a principled *difference in kind* between labour and employment issues on the one hand, and free market and free competition issues on the other hand. Both labour organization (employment procurement, Sunday work, tourist guides) and labour costs (state aid) are of an *economic nature* that includes them in the common economic market and subjects them to market and competition rules. The 'no commodity' slogan finds no adherents at the ECJ. The Court's refusal to separate labour from the Treaty's competition rules confirms and testifies to the latter's general material scope. Save express Treaty provision to the contrary, EC competition law applies to *all economic sectors and activities.* The specific nature of a given economic sector cannot exclude it *a priori* from EC competition law, even if that sector benefits from a specific EC policy that coexists with the EC's competition policy. That is the rule for the transport, energy, banking and insurance sectors, as well as for the organisation of social security.[49] It is clearly the rule that the abovementioned cases extend to the labour sector.

Second, under the all-embracing cloak of EC competition law, the specific nature of the labour sector may justify a tailored accommodation to protect the legitimate aims pursued by the measure at hand. Whereas labour does not present a difference in kind that exempts it from competition law, its specific nature may therefore lead to a *difference in degree* in the application of that law.

What is true for labour and employment issues in general seems equally true for collective bargaining and collective labour agreements in particular. Although the reported cases do not consider this particular issue directly and explicitly, they tellingly contain no special consideration where collective labour relations are indeed involved. The seminal *Albany* case would change all that.

---

[48] ECJ 5 June 1997, *Ypourgos Ergasias*, C-398/95, (1997) *E.C.R.* I-3091.

[49] See A.M. Van den Bossche, "CAO's en mededingingsrecht", in M. Rigaux and P. Humblet (eds.), *Actuele problemen van het arbeidsrecht 6*, Antwerpen, Intersentia, 2001, 673, at 685–686, and the many references there.

Section III. The Surprising Labour Exemption: *Albany* and Its Progeny

§ 1. A Partial Labour Exemption

17. The facts of *Albany* and its sister cases *Brentjens* and *Drijvende Bokken* need only a brief reminder here. The organization of the famed Dutch pension system allows representatives of employers and employees to create a pension fund with exclusive rights for a given sector of industry, affiliation to which is made compulsory by the Dutch government at the request of the said representatives. *Albany International BV*, *Brentjens' Handelsonderneming BV* and *BV Maatschappij Drijvende Bokken* all preferred their own supplementary pension schemes over a sectoral pension scheme which they claimed to be less generous for their workers. They opposed compulsory affiliation to the sectoral pension fund, *inter alia* on grounds of EC competition rules. In that context the ECJ was forced to consider head-on the relationship between collective labour agreements, concluded by the representatives of management and labour, and article 81 TEC.

18. Whereas Advocate-general F. Jacobs' extensive and instructive opinion had culminated in a balanced and mitigated escape from competition law intrusion, the ECJ quickly establishes a *per se* preferential status for collective labour agreements *vis-à-vis* competition rules. In true *Hegelian* style, a partial exemption of collective labour agreements from article 81 TEC is presented as the inescapable synthesis of a thesis and antithesis within the TEC.

As *thesis*, the ECJ reminds us that the activities of the Community include not only a system ensuring that competition in the internal market is not distorted (art. 3(1) g TEC), but also a policy in the social sphere, aimed at promoting a harmonious and balanced development of economic activities, and a high level of employment and of social protection (art. 2 TEC). In that connection it refers to the Treaty's promotion of collective bargaining, especially the possibility for management and labour to form contractual relations, including agreements (art. 138–139 TEC).

As *antithesis*, the ECJ then emphatically declares it to be 'beyond question that certain restrictions of competition are inherent in collective agreements between organizations representing employers and workers'. Therefore, the social policy objectives pursued by such agreements would be seriously undermined if management and labour were to be subjected to article 81(1) TEC 'when seeking jointly to adopt measures to improve conditions of work and employment'.

It therefore follows, as *synthesis*, 'from an interpretation of the provisions of the Treaty as a whole which is both effective and consistent that agreements concluded in the context of collective negotiations between management and labour in pursuit of such objectives must, by virtue of their nature and purpose, be regarded as falling outside the scope of article 81(1) of the Treaty'.[50]

19. *Albany* and co's partial exemption of collective labour agreements from article 81(1) TEC was quickly confirmed in another set of Dutch cases, *Pavlov* and *van der Woude*. Turning *Albany*'s analysis into a standard formula, both these succeeding cases remind us 'that agreements concluded in the context of collective bargaining between employers and employees and aimed at improving employment conditions are not, by reason of their nature and purpose, to be regarded as falling within the scope of article 81(1) of the Treaty'.[51] These agreements' immunity from competition law remains embedded in their connection with the social policy of the EC, and in the Treaty's encouragement of social dialogue, including genuine agreements. Parties or agreements that do not fit into that mould do not escape EC competition law.[52]

In the perceived field of tension between the EC's economic aims, for which free competition is instrumental, and the EC's social policy which supports the negotiation of collective labour agreements, the ECJ therefore gives precedence to the social over the economic. *Albany* and its progeny symbolically contradict the traditionally assumed primacy of the economic in the European integration process.[53] They are moreover the first, and so far only cases, where the ECJ has self-imposed a categorical limitation to the material scope of EC competition law.[54] Before delineating the exact contours of this limitation, its justification in principle needs to be examined.

---

[50] ECJ 21 September 1999, *Albany*, C-67/96, (1999) *E.C.R.* I-5751, para. 57–60; ECJ 21 September 1999, *Brentjens*, C-115/97 through C-117/97, (1999) *E.C.R.* I-6025, para. 51–57; ECJ 21 September 1999, *Drijvende Bokken*, C-219/97, (1999) *E.C.R.* I-6121, para. 41–47; comp. F. Jacobs' opinion in *Albany*, *Brentjens*, and *Drijvende Bokken*, respectively C-67/96, joined cases C-115/97, C-116/97, C-117/97, and C-219/97, (1999) *E.C.R.* I-5751, VI-B-2-b.

[51] ECJ 12 September 2000, *Pavlov*, C-180/98 through C-184/98, (2000) *E.C.R.* I-6451, para. 67; ECJ 21 September 2000, *van der Woude*, C-222/98, (2000) *E.C.R.* I-7111, para. 22.

[52] ECJ 12 September 2000, *Pavlov*, C-180/98 through C-184/98, (2000) *E.C.R.* I-6451, para. 69–70; A.M. Van den Bossche, "CAO's en mededingingsrecht", n. 49 above, at 704–706.

[53] M. De Vos, "De Europese CAO", n. 1 above, at 20.

[54] See A.M. Van den Bossche, "CAO's en mededingingsrecht", n. 49 above, at 723.

§ 2. A Fundamental Critique of Albany

1. Incorrect Premises

20. Even a superficial reading of *Albany* highlights the weakness of the premises that underlay the ECJ's reasoning. Confronted with *Dutch* cases and *Dutch* collective agreements, the ECJ builds up a labour exemption from the recognition of the ... *European* social dialogue in the TEC. Article 139(1) TEC's confirmation that the dialogue between management and labour at the Community level may lead to contractual relations, including agreements, is used to create an exemption which saves the Dutch collective agreements from the claws of EC competition law. However, if article 139(1) TEC is indeed to imply an exemption of collective labour agreements from EC competition law, it can clearly only exempt the agreements mentioned therein, i.e. the *European* collective labour agreements concluded by management and labour at the Community level.[55] Moreover, only collective labour agreements that are either concluded at the Community level or implement community policy at the national level can be connected to the EC's social policy goals, a connection which the ECJ invokes to justify the exemption from EC competition law.[56] The support and organization of the European social dialogue in the TEC therefore cannot *per se* be extended to the purely national social dialogue, as the ECJ seems to do.

The technical inadequacy of the ECJ's premises is compounded by a more fundamental one. As we have seen, the Court begins its analysis by acknowledging *a priori* an inherent conflict between competition and collective labour agreements: 'It is beyond question that certain restrictions of competition are inherent in collective agreements between organizations representing employers and workers'. For the ECJ, collective agreements and free competition law necessarily collide. The Court therefore submits to a *unidimensional view of competition law* as guaranteeing effective free competition. In that dimension, competition law is indeed intrinsically incompatible with collective labour agreements, as we have seen.[57] However, EC competition law is not only aimed at assuring free and unfettered competition. It must be viewed in its context and as one of the tools for achieving the aims and objectives of the TEC. EC competition rules therefore not only preserve a competitive market economy, they also support the creation of an *integrated single market*. The additional function of *market integration* is important and sometimes overriding. It can justify

---

[55] M. De Vos, "De Europese CAO", n. 1 above, at 20; S. Vousden, "Albany, Market Law and Social Exclusion" (2000) *I.L.J.* 181, at 188.

[56] Comp. W. Berg, "Neue Entscheidungen des EuGH zur Anwendung des EG-Kartellrechts im Bereich der sozialen Sicherheit" (2000) *Eu.Z.W.* 170, at 171.

[57] *Supra*, at para. 5.

behaviour and agreements that competition rules elsewhere, not concerned with the obsession of single market unification, do not condone.[58] Therefore, the ECJ should have considered the relationship between EC competition law and collective labour agreements *from the angle of market integration* before postulating any inherent contradiction between them. It cannot be excluded that some collective labour agreements, through determination and unification of minimum labour conditions, may contribute to the integration of the single market, particularly in view of their supposed efficiency effects.[59]

2. *Unnecessary and Unjustified Labour Supremacy*

21. Even under its debatable assumptions, the extent of *Albany*'s labour exemption was neither necessary nor justified. A peek across the Atlantic shows us why. The European and American starting points are identical. The ECJ works with a Treaty which recognizes (European) collective bargaining while protecting free competition. Similarly, the American Supreme Court deals with federal legislation that recognises and supports collective bargaining – the National Labor Relations Act (NLRA) – while protecting free competition through antitrust provisions. Confronted with the coexistence of these potentially conflicting congressional policies, the US Supreme Court has created what is generally called a non-statutory labour exemption from antitrust. However, the nature of the American non-statutory 'labour exemption' fundamentally distinguishes it from its European counterpart in *Albany*.

In the supposed conflict between collective bargaining and antitrust, the US Supreme Court does not favour the one (collective bargaining) over the other (antitrust). Its purpose is not a categorical exemption, but a 'proper accommodation between the congressional policies favoring collective bargaining under the NLRA and the congressional policy favoring free competition'. This essentially shelters collective bargaining from competition law to the extent that it is *necessary to safeguard the right to collective bargaining*, i.e. for its hard core of party-to-party negotiation of wages and working conditions.[60] Advocate-general LENZ in *Bosman* and Advocate-general JACOBS in *Albany* both proposed similar solutions for the European

[58] See C. BELLAMY and G. CHILD, *European Community Law of Competition*, n. 9 above, at 40–41; A. JONES and B. SUFRIN, *EC Competition Law*, n. 9 above, at 15–17 and 30–33; R. WHISH, *Competition Law*, n. 9 above, at 19.

[59] *Supra*, at para. 2, for these supposed efficiency effects.

[60] *Connel Constr. Co. v. Plumbers*, 2 June 1975, 421 U.S. 616, at 622. For a general analysis, see D. LESLIE, "Principles of Labor Antitrust" (1980) 66 *Va. L. Rev.* 1183; M. HANDLER and W. ZIFCHAK, "Collective Bargaining and the Antitrust Laws: The Emasculation of the Labor Exemption" (1981) 81 *Colum. L. Rev.* 459.

combination of collective bargaining and competition law.[61] In their and in the American analysis, recognition of collective bargaining and protection of free competition coexist without hierarchy, excluding precedence of one over the other. Rather than truly *exempting* collective bargaining from antitrust, they actually *accommodate* an antitrust policy that remains otherwise applicable.

The EC Commission adopts a similar approach to the equally sensitive relation between *sports and competition law*. It does not apply article 81(1) TEC to rules that are inherent to sport and/or *necessary for its organisation*,[62] a view apparently supported by the ECJ's case-law.[63] In that view, a sort of proportionality test 'exempts' from article 81 those restrictions necessary and indispensable for achieving legitimate sporting goals.[64] That is the type of balancing required where no principled limitation of the Treaty's competition rules exist.

22. *Albany*, however, does not balance, it choses and prefers. In a forced and unnecessary attempt to salvage the Treaty's social policy objectives, it jettisons article 81 TEC and offers a blanket safeguard for 'agreements concluded in the context of collective bargaining between employers and employees and aimed at improving employment conditions'. In the process it establishes a factual supremacy of social dialogue (art. 138–139 TEC) over free competition (art. 81 TEC), or – as some believers frame it – a factual fundamental right to collective bargaining.[65]

The TEC evidently does not support such preferential treatment – on the contrary. Its provisions on the European social dialogue, which the ECJ uses to establish a labour exemption from competition law, are part of the chapter on social provisions. The main article of that chapter stresses 'the need to maintain the competitiveness of the Community economy' and maintains that social policy objectives will ensue partly 'from the functioning of the common market' (art. 136 TEC). Competition and common

---

[61] C. Lenz, opinion in *Bosman*, C-415/93, (1995) *E.C.R.* I-5034, para. 273–274; F. Jacobs, opinion in *Albany*, *Brentjens*, and *Drijvende Bokken*, respectively C-67/96, joined cases C-115/97, C-116/97, C-117/97, and C-219/97, (1999) *E.C.R.* I-5751, para. 190–194; comp. R. Van den Bergh and P. Camesasca, "Irreconcilable Principles? The Court of Justice Exempts Collective Labour Agreements from the Wrath of Antitrust", n. 4 above, at 500.

[62] See C. Bellamy and G. Child, *European Community Law of Competition*, n. 9 above, at 272–274.

[63] See A. Egger and C. Stix-Hackl, "Sports and Competition Law: A Never-ending Story?" (2002) *E.C.L.R.* 81, 88–89.

[64] C. Bellamy and G. Child, *European Community Law of Competition*, n. 9 above, at 274.

[65] T. Blanke, (2000) 48 *Arbeit und Recht* 30.

market are therefore an integral part of the Community's social policy, and cannot be separated from it as happens in *Albany*. The principles of the Community, set out in the initial articles of the TEC, go even further. All of the Community's purposes enumerated in art. 2 TEC, including its social policy, are to be achieved through activities which 'shall include (...) the adoption of an economic policy which is based on (...) the internal market (...), and conducted in accordance with the principle of an open market economy with free competition' (art. 4 TEC). This clearly presents the common market and its free competition as overarching goals from which no EC policy can be exempted. If any hierarchy is to be wrung from the TEC, precedence should rather go to competition policy over social policy rather than *vice versa*.[66] The naked truth, however, is that social policy and competition policy coexist as common EC objectives without a formal internal hierarchy and that the authors of the TEC, especially when developing the EC's social policy in *Maastricht* and *Amsterdam*, were apparently unaware of any potential conflict between the policies. This reality calls for a balanced *modus vivendi*, not for the partial priority of one policy over the other.[67]

3. Contentious Relationship with the Previous Case-law

23. *Albany* and its progeny comport with the existing ECJ case-law to the extent that they put collective labour relations and competition law in the same economic sphere. Their understanding of an inherent conflict between collective labour agreements and free competition indeed assumes the requisite economic nature that brings labour issues into the ambit of EC competition rules. Only by accepting the economic nature of labour issues can their settlement through collective bargaining run into EC competition law, which is restricted to economic activities. There, however, the analogy with the previous ECJ case-law ends.

24. In its earlier cases, as we have seen, the ECJ had put labour issues under the general material scope of common market and competition rules, while recognizing the possibility of a balanced accommodation in view of their legitimate aim.[68] In that vein, delineating the relationship between collective labour agreements and article 81 TEC in fact requires little creativity. The logical first step is to confront the collective labour agreement in question with article 81(1) TEC's blanket prohibition of 'all agreements

---

[66] Comp. R. Blanpain, *Europees arbeidsrecht*, Bruges, die Keure, 2001, at 80–81.
[67] M. De Vos, "De Europese CAO", n. 1 above, at 20.
[68] *Supra*, at para. 10–16.

between undertakings, decisions by associations of undertakings and concerted practices which may affect trade between Member States and which have as their object or effect the prevention, restriction or distortion of competition within the common market'. If that confrontation brings conflict – by no means the inevitable result[69] – the next step is to fathom a special nature or aim which could help to accommodate the contested labour provision. In the context of article 81 TEC that accommodation is materialized in its section three, which allows an exemption for agreements, decisions, and concerted practices that – within certain limits – contribute to improving the production or distribution of goods or to promoting technical or economic progress. Social grounds and employment concerns have been read into this statutory exemption,[70] which may also save collective labour agreements in light of their purported economic and efficiency benefits.

This orthodox and technical approach was adopted by the Commission in its decision in *Irish Banks' Standing Committee*. The Commission had to decide whether the regulation of opening hours for banks in Ireland conflicted with what is now article 81 TEC. The opening hours had been the subject of formal agreements, including agreements with the trade union of the banks' employees. Considering opening hours to be an aspect of competition between undertakings, the Commission naturally subjected the agreements to article 81 TEC scrutiny, only to find no appreciable prevention, restriction or distortion of competition.[71]

25. With and since *Albany*, the ECJ has left orthodoxy for a limited but categorical labour exemption that runs afoul of the convictions that permeate its earlier case-law. Why social policy, in the shape of collective labour agreements, deserves the exemption from competition law that the ECJ has

---

[69] A violation of article 81(1) TEC requires (i) 'undertakings' which (ii) have concluded 'agreements' that (iii) may appreciably prevent, restrict or distort competition within the common market, and (iv) may appreciably affect trade between Member States (see C. BELLAMY and G. CHILD, *European Community Law of Competition*, n. 9 above, 44 *et seq.*; A. JONES and B. SUFRIN, *EC Competition Law*, n. 9 above, 85 *et seq.*; R. WHISH, *Competition Law*, n. 9 above, 65 *et seq.*). Collective labour agreements certainly do not always or necessarily fulfil these cumulative conditions (see, e.g., F. JACOBS' opinion in *Albany*, *Brentjens*, and *Drijvende Bokken*, respectively C-67/96, joined cases C-115/97, C-116/97, C-117/97, and C-219/97, (1999) *E.C.R.* I-5751, para. 201–297).

[70] See ECJ 25 October 1975, *Metro*, 26/76, (1977) *E.C.R.* 1875, para. 43; ECJ 11 July 1985, *Remia*, 42/84, (1985) *E.C.R.* 2545, para. 42; Commission Decision 84/380/EEC of 4 July 1984, *Synthetic Fibres*, *OJ L* 207, 2 August 1984, 17, para. 37; Commission Decision 93/49/EEC of 23 December 1992, *Ford/Volkswagen*, *OJ L* 20, 28 January 1993, 14, para. 23.

[71] Commission Decision 86/507/EEC of 30 September 1986, *OJ L* 295, 18 October 1986, 28–30.

so far refused to give any other sensitive sector of an economic nature, remains a mystery. Or do *Albany* and its progeny instead herald a dramatic shift that will in due course be extended to other 'special' sectors such as environment, public health, education or consumer protection?[72] In the related context of *social security services*, for instance, the ECJ has not (yet) created a genuine exemption from competition law, but it adopts a limited 'solidarity exclusion' for compulsory social insurance services based on the solidarity principle, irrespective of their economic nature.[73]

Time will tell whether *Albany* and its immediate progeny are but an *accident de parcours*, or the dawning of a new age in the development of the EC, away from the *pensée unique* of free competition. I have merely endeavoured to demonstrate how *Albany*'s labour exemption rests upon false premises and is technically both unnecessary and unwarranted, especially considering the line of cases that preceded it. It remains now to determine the exact contours of the labour exemption as it now stands, and to sketch possible future developments under the new mantra.

§ 3. Delineating the Current Case Law

1. A General and A Limited Scope

26. As we have seen, the ECJ has so far exclusively dealt with *Dutch sectoral collective agreements*. But the immunity from competition law which the ECJ applies to those agreements is generally formulated for 'agreements concluded in the context of collective bargaining between employers and employees'. *Albany*'s labour exemption therefore seems to cover any such agreement, irrespective of its level of negotiation: plant, sector, cross-industry, transnational, or European.[74] Whatever its *level*, every collective agreement whose nature and purpose fit the requirements analysed hereunder, is *a priori* exempted from article 81 TEC.

Whether the same collective agreement is also shielded from *national* competition law is a question of the applicable national law. It remains to be seen whether the ECJ will use *Albany*'s preference for EC social policy over EC economic policy to require similar national labour exemptions for the European collective agreements that make EC social policy or for the national collective agreements that implement EC social policy at the national level.[75]

---

[72] Comp. E. Loozen, "CAO's, bedrijfspensioenfondsen en het EG-mededingingsrecht" (1999) *Nederlands Tijdschrift voor Europees Recht* 274, at 279 (affirmative); A.M. Van den Bossche, "CAO's en mededingingsrecht", n. 49 above, at 707–708 (critical).

[73] That is at least A. Winterstein's assessment: "Nailing the Jellyfish: Social Security and Competition Law" (1999) *E.C.L.R.* 324, at 327–331.

[74] M. De Vos, "De Europese CAO", n. 1 above, at 18.

[75] Art. 10 TEC would have to be the vehicle to deduce such a Member State obligation.

27. As far as EC law is concerned, *Albany*'s preferential regime for collective agreements remains limited to *article 81 TEC*. The relationship between collective bargaining and collective labour relations with the other Treaty rules on competition remains as yet unexplored, and there is now no reason or justification to stretch the labour exemption into that area. As a singular exception to, and deviation from, classic EC competition law, it cannot be extended *per analogiam*. The ECJ has itself hinted to that effect in *van der Woude*, by analysing whether the execution of the collective agreement it sheltered from article 81 TEC nonetheless amounted to abuse of a dominant position by one or more undertakings, as prohibited under article 82 TEC.[76] The intricate and controversial question of whether unions can be considered 'undertakings' for the purpose of EC competition law has therefore faded but not disappeared. Even article 81(1) TEC and its focus on undertakings retains some relevance in the context of collective labour relations. *Albany*'s labour exemption rests upon a double condition, regarding the *nature* and the *purpose* of the agreement. Agreements that do not fulfil this double condition are not sheltered from article 81 TEC scrutiny.[77]

2. The Nature of the Exempted Agreements

28. Extracted from article 81 TEC are 'agreements concluded in the context of collective bargaining between employers and employees', i.e. agreements in the *form* of collective agreements which are the *result* of collective bargaining between employers and employees. It seems irrelevant whether the employers and employees negotiate themselves or through their organizations. The case-law in its English language version mentions both, while its original Dutch version uses the more adequate and generic term 'social partners'.[78] What constitute 'agreements', 'collective bargaining' and 'social partners' or '(organizations of) employers and employees' in the sense of the labour exemption, remains largely to be determined. But there can be no doubt that these notions form genuine constitutive conditions.

29. The ECJ in *Pavlov* has refused to apply *Albany*'s labour exemption to the *liberal professions*. Members of a liberal profession are not 'employers

---

[76] ECJ 21 September 2000, *van der Woude*, C-222/98, (2000) *E.C.R.* I-7111, para. 28–30.

[77] M. De Vos, "De Europese CAO", n. 1 above, at 19; E. Franssen, A. Jacobs, A. Jaspers and K. Mortelmans, "CAO's en mededingingsrecht" (2000) *S.M.A.* 324, at 331; W. Berg, "Neue Entscheidungen des EuGH zur Anwendung des EG-Kartellrechts im Bereich der sozialen Sicherheit", n. 56 above, at 171.

[78] ECJ 21 September 1999, *Albany*, C-67/96, (1999) *E.C.R.* I-5751, para. 62; ECJ 21 September 1999, *Brentjens*, C-115/97 through C-117/97, (1999) *E.C.R.* I-6025, para. 59; ECJ 21 September 1999, *Drijvende Bokken*, C-219/97, (1999) *E.C.R.* I-6121, para. 49; ECJ 12 September 2000, *Pavlov*, C-180/98 through C-184/98, (2000) *E.C.R.* I-6451, para. 67; ECJ 21 September 2000, *van der Woude*, C-222/98, (2000) *E.C.R.* I-7111, para. 22–24.

and employees'. Their agreement to set up a pension fund is 'not concluded in the context of collective bargaining between employers and employees', and is therefore not excluded from article 81 TEC.[79] Some authors consider article 139(1) TEC's 'management and labour' to be the category of social partners which benefits from the labour exemption.[80] But the current case-law at the same time holds a wider and narrower view. The ECJ, unwittingly perhaps, goes beyond article 139(1) by extending the labour exemption to social partners involved in *national* collective bargaining, as it has consistently done in its exclusively Dutch cases. Article 139(1) TEC indeed remains limited to partners involved in a Community-level dialogue.[81] On the other hand the ECJ creates – as we shall see – an exemption for collective *labour* agreements, which only benefits the social partners involved in that type of collective bargaining. Article 139(1) TEC's notion of 'management and labour' in fact covers the diversity of social partners involved in all aspects of the Community's social policy, including but not limited to the social partners who collectively negotiate labour conditions.[82]

It remains to be seen whether the ECJ will require any guarantees for the bargaining process or for the identity of the organizations involved. Sufficient *representativeness* of the contracting parties would be an obvious angle,[83] but it is not a prerequisite that automatically follows from the ECJ's reference to the European social dialogue in articles 138–139 TEC. These articles only require a selection on grounds of representativeness when the social partners become formally involved in the realization of the Community's social policy, either through consultation (art. 138) or through implementation of their agreements (art. 139(2)). But article 139(1) TEC's autonomous recognition of the freedom to negotiate agreements extends to every possible organization.[84] If, as the ECJ erroneously believes, article 139(1) necessitates a labour exemption from article 81 TEC, then that exemption is not intrinsically limited to the agreements concluded by representative social partners.

---

[79] ECJ 12 September 2000, *Pavlov*, C-180/98 through C-184/98, (2000) *E.C.R.* I-6451, para. 68–70.

[80] E. Franssen, A. Jacobs, A. Jaspers and K. Mortelmans, "CAO's en mededingingsrecht", n. 77 above, at 332.

[81] See M. De Vos, "De Europese CAO", n. 1 above, at 22–23.

[82] See M. De Vos, "De Europese CAO", n. 1 above, at 22; contra M. LeFriant and A. Höland, "La reconnaissance des contrats collectifs par le droit communautaire", in G. Winter (ed.) *Sources and Categories of European Union Law*, Baden-Baden, Nomos, 1996, 677, at 680.

[83] E. Franssen, A. Jacobs, A. Jaspers and K. Mortelmans, "CAO's en mededingingsrecht", n. 77 above, at 332.

[84] See M. De Vos, "De Europese CAO", n. 1 above, at 23–27.

30. *Albany*'s labour exemption only applies to *agreements* in the context of collective bargaining between both sides of industry. The concept of 'agreement' must be opposed to any type of *unilateral action* such as unilateral coordination or regulation, which remains subjected to article 81 TEC until further notice. On the other hand, if the ECJ's use of article 139 TEC is again to serve as a guideline, the category of exempted agreements should not be formally limited to collective labour agreements in whatever technical sense. Article 139(1) TEC leaves the social partners free to conclude any type of agreement, whether formal or informal, normative or gentlemen's agreements, framework or detailed agreements, etc.[85] In that respect the form of the agreement seems immaterial, as long as its purpose fits the bill.

3. The Purpose of the Exempted Agreements

31. Agreements concluded in the context of collective bargaining between (organizations of) employers and employees are only exempted from article 81 TEC if and when they *intend or aim to improve employment and working conditions*.[86] Some authors merely require agreements that pursue a *social policy objective*, in the sense of the TEC.[87] That would expand the *Albany* exemption to agreements that are not aimed at improving employment and working conditions as such, but rather at promoting employment, improving living conditions, obtaining proper social protection, promoting dialogue between management and labour, developing human resources with a view to lasting high employment, or combating exclusion.[88] The existing case-law, however, clearly refers to the improvement of employment and working conditions. It cannot be extended *per analogiam* to cover other aspects of the Community's social policy.[89]

32. What constitute 'employment and working conditions' for the purpose of *Albany*'s labour exemption is crucial for its understanding. Some authors

[85] See M. De Vos, "De Europese CAO", n. 1 above, at 14.

[86] ECJ 21 September 1999, *Albany*, C-67/96 (1999) *E.C.R.* I-5751, para. 62; ECJ 21 September 1999, *Brentjens*, C-115/97 through C-117/97 (1999) *E.C.R.* I-6025, para. 56 and 60; ECJ 21 September 1999, *Drijvende Bokken*, C-219/97 (1999) *E.C.R.* I-6121, para. 46 and 50; ECJ 12 September 2000, *Pavlov*, C-180/98 through C-184/98 (2000) *E.C.R.* I-6451, para. 67; ECJ 21 September 2000, *van der Woude*, C-222/98 (2000) *E.C.R.* I-7111, para. 22.

[87] E. Loozen, "CAO's, bedrijfspensioenfondsen en het EG-mededingingsrecht", note 72 above, at 278; A.M. Van den Bossche, "CAO's en mededingingsrecht", n. 49 above, at 702.

[88] See art. 136 TEC.

[89] M. De Vos, "De Europese CAO", n. 1 above, at 19; see *supra*, para. 26.

suggest an interpretation under national law,[90] whereas others search for comparable notions in secondary Community law.[91] However interesting and inspiring, these exercises remain essentially hypothetical and prospective in the absence of explicative ECJ case-law. Advocate-general JACOBS' opinion in *Albany* seems a better guide. He advocated limiting the scope of collective bargaining immunity to core subjects as wages and working conditions, which do not directly affect third parties or markets. The test should be whether the agreement merely modifies or establishes rights and obligations within the labour relationship between employers and employees, or whether it goes beyond that and directly affects relations between employers and third parties.[92] The ECJ is unsurprisingly briefer, but its systematic reference to 'employment and/or working conditions' essentially boils down to the same thing. Employment and working conditions evidently are the rights and obligations *within the context of the employment relationship*.[93] Only collective *labour* agreements which determine such rights and obligations can benefit from *Albany*'s labour exemption.

This is an important caveat. However symbolic the creation of a preferential labour exemption from competition law may be, its *material scope* – at least at the outset – does not go beyond what accommodation without exemption would have yielded. There too, the hard core of party-to-party negotiation of wages and working conditions would have been sheltered from competition law.[94] Arrangements that do not concern the actual working and employment conditions of workers, in principle do not benefit from the labour exemption as it stands today, unless by exception and through the back door of party purpose, as we shall soon see.

33. The umbrella of 'working and employment conditions' certainly covers issues such as wages, fringe benefits, working time, schooling, job security, dismissal rules, holiday, illness and other suspensions, in short: the *individual employment relationship* between employer and employee. Relations with *third parties* such as clients, suppliers, competitors, consumers, insurers, or subcontractors are certainly not part of that equation. Collective agreements

---

[90] P. HUMBLET and M. RIGAUX, "Collective Agreements and Competition Law in Belgium", in N. BRUUN and J. HELLSTEN (eds.), *Collective Agreements and Competition Law in the EU*, Kopenhagen, DJØF Publishing, 2001, 95, at 99–100.

[91] E. FRANSSEN, A. JACOBS, A. JASPERS and K. MORTELMANS, "CAO's en mededingingsrecht", n. 77 above, at 331.

[92] F. JACOBS' opinion in *Albany, Brentjens*, and *Drijvende Bokken*, respectively C-67/96, joined cases C-115/97, C-116/97, C-117/97, and C-219/97, (1999) *E.C.R.* I-5751, para. 193.

[93] M. DE VOS, "De Europese CAO", n. 1 above, at 19. The ECJ therefore does not consider *pension rights* or *health care* as working conditions: they only directly affect a working condition, namely remuneration: *infra*, para. 35.

[94] See *supra*, para. 21.

that directly regulate such relations do not benefit from our labour exemption.[95] However, the labour exemption comes into play once the collective agreement is aimed at improving working conditions, even if that *implies third parties as an indirect by-product*. For instance, an agreement on occupational health care insurance aims to improve working conditions and is therefore shielded from article 81 TEC,[96] even if the social partners for its implementation create a separate body which has recourse to another insurer.[97]

To what extent *collective relations* between management and workers or their representatives can be considered exempted 'employment conditions', is unclear and will have to be judged on a case-by-case basis. In labour law jargon: *Albany*'s labour exemption certainly covers the individual normative part of collective labour agreements, but not necessarily the collective normative part of such agreements.[98] The position of unions, the organization of union membership, the status of union representatives, the procedure for collective action including strikes, to name but a few, are not necessarily or entirely 'employment conditions' that benefit from our labour exemption.

So called 'enriched' collective labour agreements, i.e. agreements which also deal with non-labour issues such as the environment, investment, economic development, product quality etc., clearly go beyond the material scope of a *labour* exemption, at least to their enriched *non-labour* extent.[99] As collective labour agreements often combine different types of clauses, their exemption from article 81 TEC will have to be considered on the merits of every contentious clause and can only cover the parts that aim to improve genuine employment conditions.

34. An understanding of what constitute 'employment or working conditions' is necessary but insufficient to determine the scope of *Albany*'s labour

---

[95] An agreement on *working time*, for instance, may benefit from the labour exemption, whereas an agreement on *opening hours* will not. Working time concerns the employment relation, opening hours determine relations with third parties such as contractors, clients, and consumers: comp. R. Van den Bergh and P. Camesasca, "Irreconcilable Principles? The Court of Justice Exempts Collective Labour Agreements from the Wrath of Antitrust", n. 4 above, at 496.

[96] See *infra*, para. 35.

[97] ECJ 21 September 2000, *van der Woude*, C-222/98, (2000) *E.C.R.* I-7111, para. 20 and 26.

[98] The classic distinction between individual normative stipulations and collective normative stipulations of a collective labour agreement is also maintained in the context of the EC social dialogue: C. Barnard, *EC Employment Law*, n. 3 above, at 557; R. Blanpain, *Europees arbeidsrecht*, n. 66 above, at 453.

[99] Comp. E. Franssen, A. Jacobs, A. Jaspers and K. Mortelmans, "CAO's en mededingingsrecht", n. 77 above, at 331.

exemption. As we have seen, the ECJ shields collective agreements that 'seek', 'intend' or are 'aimed at' the improvement of employment and working conditions. This constant reference to the *intentions or purposes of the agreement* has, in my view, both a restrictive and an expansive effect.

The *restrictive effect* comes into play for those collective agreements whose subject matter is indeed the improvement of employment and working conditions. Since 'purpose' is our focus, subject matter alone does not bring the labour exemption into play. The improvement of employment and working conditions must *moreover* be the *preponderant aim* of the contracting parties. Agreements which apparently deal with employment conditions but merely function as a cover to restrict competition on the market for goods and services are not protected by the labour exemption.[100] Where the indirect effect of employment conditions on the economic market becomes the parties' dominating aim, the freedom to negotiate collective labour agreements is abused for an economic aim that requires submission to competition law scrutiny. To square collective labour agreements with article 81 TEC, courts therefore cannot stop at objective contents but must push beyond for the parties' dominant subjective intentions.

35. On the other hand, the emphasis on the parties' purpose protects agreements without requiring an *effective improvement* of employment conditions. For the labour exemption to apply, it suffices that the collective agreement is *concluded* for the improvement of working conditions. It only needs to be *intended* for such improvement, irrespective of the actual realization of that intention.[101]

Moreover, and more importantly, since aim and purpose suffice, collective agreements may benefit from our labour exemption *even without directly regulating employment conditions themselves.* Collective agreements can be sheltered from article 81 TEC *merely by contributing to the improvement of working conditions*, if that improvement is their dominant purpose. That is the Court's message on agreements to create and organize a pension scheme for a given sector. These agreements, the Court notes, guarantee a certain level of pension for all workers in the sector. In so doing, they 'contribute

---

[100] Comp. F. JACOBS' opinion in *Albany*, *Brentjens*, and *Drijvende Bokken*, respectively C-67/96, joined cases C-115/97, C-116/97, C-117/97, and C-219/97, (1999) *E.C.R.* I-5751, para. 192, which draws from a comparative analysis of the competition laws of several Member States, notably Germany.

[101] See M. DE VOS, "De Europese CAO", n. 1 above, at 19; comp. W. BERG, "Neue Entscheidungen des EuGH zur Anwendung des EG-Kartellrechts im Bereich der sozialen Sicherheit", n. 56 above, at 171.

directly to improving one of their working conditions, namely their remuneration'.[102] Pension rights themselves are therefore not working conditions, but their regulation directly contributes to the improvement of a working condition, namely remuneration. The requisite *purpose* to improve working conditions thus inferred, the labour exemption comes into play.[103] Similarly, an agreement to establish an occupational health care insurance scheme in a given sector 'contributes to improving the working conditions of the employees, (...) by reducing the costs which, in the absence of a collective agreement, would have to be borne by the employees'. It too therefore has the required purpose to improve employment and working conditions.[104]

Through the focus on the agreement's *purpose*, the ECJ therefore opens the back door of its labour exemption to those collective agreements that cannot enter through the front door. Even if your object is not the improvement of employment and working conditions as such, you may still be exempted from article 81 TEC by *contributing* to such improvement. This startling extension of our labour exemption's material scope provokes two remarks. First, as for the agreements that do directly regulate employment conditions, this extended category of agreements can only benefit from the labour exemption if the parties' *dominant intention* is indeed the improvement of employment conditions. A contribution to such improvement merely gives the objective contents of the agreement, not its subjective purpose.[105] Since the object of the agreement is not the regulation of employment conditions as such, the subjective purpose of the parties will require closer attention here. Second, the ECJ only extends the labour exemption to collective agreements that contribute *directly* to the improvement of an actual working condition, *in casu* remuneration. A direct causal link is required. Agreements with only an indirect effect on employment conditions remain fully subjected to EC competition law. The exemption from article 81 TEC is and remains a *labour* exemption. Its back door stands ajar only for collective agreements that, irrespective of their different subject matter, nonetheless directly contribute to the improvement of working and employment conditions.

---

[102] ECJ 21 September 1999, *Albany*, C-67/96, (1999) *E.C.R.* I-5751, para. 63; ECJ 21 September 1999, *Brentjens*, C-115/97 through C-117/97, (1999) *E.C.R.* I-6025, para. 60; ECJ 21 September 1999, *Drijvende Bokken*, C-219/97, (1999) *E.C.R.* I-6121, para. 50; ECJ 12 September 2000, *Pavlov*, C-180/98 through C-184/98, (2000) *E.C.R.* I-6451, para. 68.

[103] M. De Vos, "De Europese CAO", n. 1 above, at 20.

[104] ECJ 21 September 2000, *van der Woude*, C-222/98, (2000) *E.C.R.* I-7111, para. 25.

[105] See *supra*, para. 34.

Section IV. Possible Future Developments

36. The previous section has amply demonstrated how both the fundamentals and the contours of the existing case-law scream for further reflection and additional cases. In this section, I shall briefly highlight other intriguing issues that may arise from the combination of the two underlying premises of *Albany* and its current progeny: (i) collective labour relations are part of the Community's economic order, and (ii) collective bargaining inherently conflicts with that order's principle of free competition, only to be saved through a limited labour exemption. These two premises frame collective labour relations and EC competition law into a *conflictual model*, of which the status of collective labour agreements is just one of the possible spinoffs.

37. For the *social partners* as such, competition law concerns do not end with the status of their collective agreements under article 81 TEC. Considering the voluntary nature of the collective bargaining process, powerful organizations can combine to exclude others. Collective labour agreements are generally concluded among the few while destined to govern all, often aided by the state intervention discussed hereunder. In that context, the question may or should arise whether the behaviour of social partner organizations, unions in particular, can constitute an abuse of a dominant position within the meaning of *article 82* of the TEC.[106] Irrespective of the technical intricacies of article 82's material scope, everything first hinges on whether, or when unions can be called 'undertakings' in EC competition law. By virtue of its labour exemption, the ECJ in *Albany* was able partially to dodge this sensitive issue as regards article 81 of the TEC.[107] It seems bound to retake the stage full and centre, divisively and provocatively, in the context of article 82 of the TEC.

One may also wonder if the economic gaze with which the ECJ contemplates collective labour relations will stretch so far as to include that other holy attribute of union activity: collective action, including strikes. Besides the contentious relationship of some forms of collective action with free movement in a common market, an intrepid reading of *Albany*'s conflictual model forces the question of whether collective action organized by or between unions can either lead to an abuse of a dominant position under article 82 TEC, or constitute an unlawful 'decision' or 'concerted practice' under article 81 TEC. How unions relate to the competition law concepts

---

[106] E. Franssen, A. Jacobs, A. Jaspers and K. Mortelmans, "CAO's en mededingingsrecht", n. 77 above, at 332.

[107] See *supra*, para. 27.

of 'undertaking' and 'association of undertakings' is also the starting point of that inquiry.

38. *Albany*'s conflictual approach to collective labour relations and EC competition law may also have collateral implications for *Member States* which are themselves involved in the collective bargaining process. We are not concerned here with the state as employer, i.e. the state as a genuine social partner in the collective bargaining process itself. In that capacity the state's position needs not in principle to be distinguished from that of the social partners discussed above. Rather, our focus here is on state intervention *from the outside*, in support of collective bargaining between the social partners.

A classic example of such state support is the selection of so-called *representative unions*. In this context, a state typically selects a limited number of organizations as preferential social partners and supports their collective bargaining. In effect, if not in theory, the selected organizations require a monopoly or oligopoly for negotiating labour conditions, to the detriment of the organizations that fail to receive the state's backing. Wherever a system of representative unions exists, the non-representative unions rebel against it: at the ILO, at the European social dialogue, and at the national level. Although these legal battles have generated some guidelines for the selection of representative unions and the exclusion of non-representative unions, none have succeeded in discrediting the system of representative unions as such.[108]

EC competition law may perhaps be the last resort for organizations fighting for survival against state-supported representative unions. The questions are then whether a state-organized system of representative unions amounts to article 86 TEC's 'special or exclusive rights for undertakings' and if so, whether these rights square with all of the Treaty's competition rules, in particular the article 82 prohibition to abuse a dominant position. Article 86 TEC requires 'Member States' – construed broadly to include any body that is a manifestation of the state – to refrain from enacting or maintaining in force any 'measure' – construed broadly to include all instruments from a public authority – contrary to EC competition rules for undertakings. In particular, Member States must refrain from

---

[108] For a general overview, see F. Dorssemont, "Representativiteit, syndicale gelijkheid en syndicale vrijheid: een met de nodige discretie verteld verhaal over een turbulente driehoeksverhouding" (1994) *Tijdschrift voor Sociaal Recht* 63, at 79–96, and his comparative analysis in F. Dorssemont, *Rechtspositie en syndicale actievrijheid van representatieve werknemersorganisaties*, Bruges, die Keure, 2002, at 213–241.

For the issue in the context of the European social dialogue, see M. De Vos, "De Europese CAO", n. 1 above, at 23–27; E. Franssen, *Legal Aspects of the European Social Dialogue*, n. 30 above, at 83–91 and 192–199.

granting special rights if the beneficiary undertakings are thereby led to abuse a dominant position or when these rights are liable to create such an abuse.[109] Here too, the primary and inescapable issue is whether or when social partner organizations that benefit from the recognition as a representative organization can be regarded as 'undertakings' for the purpose of EC competition law.

39. Another, and perhaps more obvious target of state support is the practice, institutionalized in many EC Member States, of giving *regulatory effect* to collective agreements concluded by selected social partners. The state then intervenes *ex post* to extend *erga omnnes* the effect of agreements that would otherwise have a more limited force.[110] From the angle of competition law, and in *Albany*'s conflictual vision, these state interventions enhance the competition-restrictive effects intrinsic to the collective labour agreements concerned. This raises three fundamental questions.

First, as with state recognitions of representative unions as such, state enforcement of collective labour agreements must be confronted with the Member State duty to refrain from granting special rights to undertakings in violation of the Treaty's competition rules (article 86 TEC). Giving *erga omnes* effect to collective agreements obviously strengthens the position of the signatory parties and is often linked with their recognition as representative organizations. Moreover, if the *contents* of a given collective agreement favours a particular undertaking, state enforcement of the agreement may amount to a granting of special rights inducive to abuse of a dominant position by that undertaking. That is precisely the issue in the Dutch pension fund cases in *Albany* and beyond, where collective agreements create a compulsory pension fund which obtains a monopoly through state enforcement of the collective agreements.[111]

40. Second, consistent ECJ case-law combines the Treaty's competition rules with the loyalty duty under article 10 TEC to require Member States not to introduce or maintain in force measures which may render ineffective the competition rules applicable to undertakings only. Like article 86 TEC,

---

[109] See C. Bellamy and G. Child, *European Community Law of Competition*, n. 9 above, 998–1016; A. Jones and B. Sufrin, *EC Competition Law*, n. 9 above, 429–473; R. Whish, *Competition Law*, n. 9 above, 189–210.

[110] The implementation of the European collective agreements through Council 'decision' (art. 139(2) TEC) is a similar system, and one inspired by the Member State tradition of extension *erga omnes*: see M. De Vos, "De Europese CAO", n. 1 above, at 28–31.

[111] See A.M. Van den Bossche, "CAO's en mededingingsrecht", n. 49 above, at 713–720.

article 10 TEC is a *renvoi* provision, a reference rule that requires Member States to abstain from enacting or enforcing rules which could jeopardize the effectiveness of the Treaty's rules on competition between undertakings.[112] The second question, therefore, is whether state enforcement of collective labour agreements may run afoul of the state's loyalty duty *vis-à-vis* competition rules, given *Albany*'s assumption of an inherent conflict between collective labour agreements and free competition.[113]

Under the ECJ's case-law as it stands, state support for a private agreement is not contrary to article 10 *juncto* 81 of the TEC if the *agreement itself* is compatible with article 81(1).[114] The automatic link between the legality of a private agreement and a state measure that generates or extends the agreement's competition restrictive effects has been convincingly criticized without altering the course of the ECJ.[115] Accordingly, collective agreements that fall within the scope of *Albany*'s labour exemption can safely be enforced through state intervention even if that enforcement exasperates their anti-competitive effects.[116] Member States are consequently home free, as long as they aptly verify the respect of EC competition rules, including whether the agreement presented for enforcement is indeed covered by *Albany*'s labour exemption. But that's not the end of the line.

41. Member States' loyalty duty towards EC competition rules has another consequence which has so far remained unexplored. Settled ECJ case-law holds articles 10 *juncto* 81 of the TEC to be infringed where a Member State 'divests its own rules of the character of legislation by delegating to private economic operators responsibility for taking decisions affecting the economic sphere'.[117] A Member State may not delegate to 'private economic operators' the power to take collective decisions concerning economic matters, except where legislation ensures that the private operators in fact

---

[112] See C. Bellamy and G. Child, *European Community Law of Competition*, n. 9 above, at 838–842; R. Whish, *Competition Law*, n. 9 above, at 184–189.

[113] For an analysis prior to *Albany*, see S. Graf von Wallwitz, *Tarifverträge und die Wettbewerbsordnung des EG-Vertrages*, n. 29 above, at 200–226.

[114] ECJ 18 June 1998, *Corsica Ferries*, C-266/96, (1998) E.C.R. I-3949, para. 51; R. Whish, *Competition Law*, n. 9 above, at 188–189.

[115] See F. Jacobs' opinion in *Pavlov*, joined cases C-180/98 to C-184/98, (2000) *E.C.R.* I-6451, para. 160–165.

[116] ECJ 21 September 1999, *Albany*, C-67/96, (1999) *E.C.R.* I-5751, para. 66; ECJ 21 September 1999, *Brentjens*, C-115/97 through C-117/97, (1999) *E.C.R.* I-6025, para. 66; ECJ 21 September 1999, *Drijvende Bokken*, C-219/97, (1999) *E.C.R.* I-6121, para. 56; A.M. Van den Bossche, "CAO's en mededingingsrecht", n. 49 above, at 721–722.

[117] See, *inter alia*, ECJ 21 September 1988, *Van Eycke*, 267/86, (1988) *E.C.R.* 4769, para. 16; ECJ 17 November 1993, *Reiff*, C-185/91, (1993) *E.C.R.* I-5801, para. 14; ECJ 5 October 1995, *Centro Servizi Spediporto*, C-96/94, (1995) *E.C.R.* I-2883, para. 21; ECJ 19 February 2002, *Arduino*, C-35/99, (2002) *E.C.R.*, I-1529, para. 35.

have to operate like an arm of the state by taking the public interest into account.[118] Since the ECJ consistently sees labour issues as economic issues,[119] the social partners' autonomy to bargain collectively on labour issues needs to be examined. Do Member States fail their loyalty duty with regard to EC competition law when they leave it to private organizations to settle labour issues collectively in their interest or give *erga omnes* effect to freely negotiated collective labour agreements? The issue is as evident as it is surprising, and it symbolically pits competition law against the sacred freedom to bargain collectively, both of which are supported by the TEC itself. It looks like *Albany* all over again.

CONCLUSION

42. The story of collective labour agreements and EC competition law remains largely to be discovered. After the initial breakthrough of *Albany* and the immediately succeeding cases, a surprising radio silence has set in. The issue still does not seem to have fully penetrated the practitioner's mind. *Albany* so far has remained a symbol rather than a watershed, an eccentric rather than a seminal case. That may and should change. Our analysis has revealed many an open question and plenty of room for debate. The merits of *Albany*'s labour exemption require new and further scrutiny. In my opinion, the creation of a non-statutory labour exemption from EC competition law is both unnecessary and unjustified.

Subject to a surprising reversal at the ECJ, however, social partners organizations can boast their immunity from EC competition law as they engage in collective bargaining. But their victory is only partial, perhaps even pyrrhic. *Albany*'s labour exemption in essence does not go beyond what accommodation without exemption would have tolerated, and yet it does so at the price of including collective bargaining into the organization of the common economic market and by recognizing an inherent conflict between them. That may turn out to be a high price indeed, since it provokes new issues of compatibility between collective bargaining and the Treaty's competition rules. *Albany* in all likelihood was but the initial battle, however important, in a longer campaign. The premises underpinning its partial labour exemption may eventually backfire on the now victorious social partners and on the Member States. Only the future will tell whether the ECJ, when confronted anew with the relationship between collective bargaining and EC competition law, will return to orthodoxy or will instead further erode the free competition backbone of the common market.

---

[118] See C. BELLAMY and G. CHILD, *European Community Law of Competition*, n. 9 above, at 840–841; R. WHISH, *Competition Law*, n. 9 above, at 187–188.

[119] Both before and in *Albany*: see *supra*, para. 11–16 and 23.

Part Two
Management and Labour

Chapter Four
Social Dialogue – an ETUC Perspective

Penny Clarke

Introduction

1. The invitation for this meeting says that the 'initial dreams' regarding the development of a European social dialogue 'have all but evaporated'.

This prompts two initial reflections: why is it always easier to criticize what has *not* been achieved than to measure what has? And what would Europe be like without the European social dialogue?

On the first point, although the European social dialogue is far from perfect, it is actually quite surprising that we have managed to build (or start to build) a European system of industrial relations, given the diversity in our different countries, and the relative newness of EU social dialogue, and indeed of EU social policy.

Nonetheless, we know that we face many challenges, and indeed the social partners' Laeken Declaration recognizes that it is an appropriate moment to take stock of both bipartite social dialogue and tripartite social concertation.

EU Social Dialogue – Part of the European Social Model

2. First however, we point out that the social dialogue is part of our social and economic model. The model, which is of course not static but evolving, is based on the recognition that:

- social and economic progress are friends, not enemies;
- the invisible hand of the market has to be balanced by the visible hand of government;
- in the final analysis, economic and social life – as political life – must be democratic and therefore people-centred.

All European countries have, relative to most other parts of the world

- high levels of social protection;

– well-developed systems of social partnership and collective bargaining;
– strong traditions of public service (services of general interest).

Trade unions have fought hard for the process of European integration to have these social characteristics. As well as being important in their own right, they undoubtedly also contribute to the economic performance of the European Union. The growing importance of sustainable development strategies will reinforce the need for a social dimension.

Finally, by being European and not just national, the model is stronger and capable of internal renewal.

ETUC/UNICE-UEAPME/CEEP Agreements: Minimum Rights Which Form Part of the 'Acquis Communautaire'

3. In terms of the agreements negotiated to date the ETUC has tried to contribute to social Europe. Let us look at the agreements:

- parental leave agreement (1996): minimum requirement for an individual, non-transferable right to parental leave (3 months) and urgent family leave;
- part-time agreement (1997): principle of non-discrimination, development of 'quality' part-time work, recognition of problems in relation to social security;
- fixed-term work agreement (1999): affirmation that permanent contracts are the rule, principle of non-discrimination, regulation as a European principle (with open list of choices), recognition of problems in relation to social security, including complementary pensions;
- temporary agency work agreement – failure March 2001 – Directive?
- framework of actions on life-long learning (2002): the social partners' 'open method of coordination' (OMC) agreement fixing objectives for national or sectorial-level implementation;
- telework agreement (2002): first 'voluntary' agreement which is binding on our respective affiliates and will be implemented in collective agreements (This should be a test of our relationship with our affiliates. When the employers negotiated on 'pay' in the part-time and fixed-term agreements, some of them went home and argued that the agreements did not include pay at all ...). For the ETUC the telework agreement is a key development because we want to develop our capacity to conclude agreements with employers at European level.

4. The ETUC would have liked to negotiate more (EWCs, sexual harassment, information and consultation ...) but nonetheless, is the record so meagre? We've also said that other action by the social partners is important ('factors of success', common opinions, support for social partners in the candidate countries). Of course, it is important not only to negotiate agreements but also to implement them in practice. We miss information on the impact of our first agreement (the report of the Commission leaves a lot to be desired) but the ETUC does, with the help of ETUI, provide this, and the results so far have proved positive.

In addition, the result of the *sectorial dialogue* should also be considered when evaluating the EU social dialogue over the last 10 years or so. As well as 'legislative' agreements regarding excluded sectors in the working time Directive (civil aviation and maritime transport) there are 27 or so sectorial committees (new arrangements 1999). There are many interesting joint texts (agreements on telework in telecoms and commerce sectors; codes of practice on fundamental rights in textiles, shoe sectors; manual on tenders in private security; good practice training, equality ...). In future the *sectorial*-level dialogue will play an increasing role (technological change, work organization, restructuring ...).

Furthermore, the company level and the dialogue developed in the 800+ *EWCs* is also relevant.

Last but not least, the *cross-border dimension* is a potential area for the development of social dialogue (not least in light of the growing regional disparities in employment identified in the 2002 Employment report of the Commission). The ETUC supports nearly 50 Interregional Trade Union Committees (ITUCs) which provide practical information to cross-border workers (tax, social security) and are linked to EURES. Some of these have the beginnings of a dialogue with employers in these regions.

THE SOCIAL PARTNERS' LAEKEN DECLARATION DECEMBER 2001

5. The Declaration clarified the different forms of 'dialogue': consultation, tripartism, bipartism, and aimed at supporting a better integration of the different areas of tripartite concertation (employment, macroeconomic, social protection) through the setting up of a Committee (or Summit) for concertation and employment (which needs a decision by the Danish presidency). This also supports the objectives of the Governance White Paper.

In our text we agreed to establish a multi-annual work programme for the social dialogue, taking into account Social Agenda and Lisbon strategy (ETUC demand since 1998) and to have regular social dialogue summits to agree and evaluate such a programme.

For the ETUC such a work programme is not instead of the Commission activity, but in complement to it.

Nor will it mean that we will not do anything if it is not in the programme.

The ETUC would have liked to go a bit further and to raise the issue of an independent social dialogue secretariat to support the implementation of the work programme, but this was seen as premature.

The content of the work programme will be agreed at the social dialogue summit on 28 November.

Even if we cannot talk about the content of the social dialogue work programme today, what is important to note is that the programme should build a dynamic between the EU and national level and contain a wide range of proposed instruments, including binding agreements.

Finally, there is a growing link – which needs to be developed – between the actions of the social partners in social dialogue, the European Employment Strategy (EES), and EU coordination of collective bargaining. Quality of employment is a central ETUC objective here. We can take the example of equal pay: this is an issue for the social dialogue and for the EES (and indeed for EU legislation).

The Need for Greater Social and Economic Convergence

6. Enlargement demands greater progress on strategies aimed at social and economic convergence.

This means countering the agenda of those who say that it is not possible to have any more EU social policy (because the differences between countries will be too wide) or indeed want to promote deregulation. While it is true that the OMC etc are interesting and innovative ways of promoting convergence, this does not mean that minimum standards – both legislation and collective agreements – no longer have any place. However, in any event, whether legislation, agreements or OMC, what is important is to see the tangible results in practice.

In the area of social dialogue and collective bargaining, it is important that employers recognize the interest of having collective frameworks. Employers need fair competition and a level playing field in employment conditions; they also need investment in 'common goods' such as education and training in order to have qualified, competent workers; they also benefit from having a stable workforce and industrial peace. For small companies in particular collective frameworks regulating employment conditions are particularly important. Hence there is a real need to ensure that strategies for convergence are indeed articulated at all levels, and by all actors.

European Trade Union Confederation (ETUC)*
Union of Industrial and Employers' Confederations of Europe (UNICE)
European Centre of Enterprises with Public Participation and of Enterprises of General Economic Interest (CEEP)

28 November 2002

Work programme of the European social partners

1. Introduction

Concerned to play their role to the full, ETUC, CEEP and UNICE/UEAPME affirmed their intention to develop a work programme for a more autonomous social dialogue in the joint declaration to the Laeken European Council in December 2001.

Conscious that development of the European social dialogue presupposes strong involvement of national employer and trade union leaders, CEEP, UNICE/UEAPME and ETUC are pleased to present their work programme on the occasion of the social dialogue summit, in Brussels on 28 November 2002, bringing together the social partners of 30 European countries: the 15 Member States of the European Union, the 2 countries which constitute with them the European Economic Area and the 13 candidate countries.

This work programme, to be carried out over the years 2003, 2004 and 2005, is built on a spectrum of diversified instruments and comprises a balanced range of themes of common interest for employers and workers.

Wishing their work programme to make a useful contribution to the Lisbon European strategy, as well as to the preparation of enlargement, UNICE/UEAPME, CEEP and ETUC have decided to group their actions around three big priorities: employment, mobility and enlargement.

---

* With the Liaison Committee Eurocadres/CEC.

Chapters	Themes	Actions	Calendar
Employment	*Employment guidelines*	Reports on SP actions in MS to implement employment guidelines (taking into account the cycle of 3 years)	2003–2005
	Lifelong learning	Follow-up of "framework of actions" + Evaluation report	2003–2005
	Stress at work:	Seminar in view of negotiating a voluntary agreement	2003
	Gender equality	Seminar on equal opportunities and gender discrimination aiming at a framework of actions	2003
	Restructuring	Identify orientations that could serve as a reference to assist in managing change and its social consequences on the basis of concrete cases, using the methodology of the Knokke seminar	2003
	Disability	Update of joint declaration of 1999 as a contribution for the European year on disability	2003–2005
	Young people	Promoting young people's interest in science and technology to help addressing the skills gap through joint declaration and/or awareness-raising campaign	2004
	Racism	Updating joint declaration of 1995 (with participation of candidate countries)	2004
	Ageing workforce	Seminar to discuss case studies and explore possible joint actions	2004–2005
	Harassment	Seminar to explore possibility of negotiating a voluntary agreement	2004
	Telework	Monitoring of follow-up to framework agreement	2004–2005
	Undeclared work	Seminar aiming at a joint opinion	2003–2005

Continued

Enlargement (follow up to Bratislava)	*Industrial relations*	Joint seminars on industrial relations (case studies on different ways of articulating different levels of negotiations)	2005
	Social dialogue	2 enlarged SDC per year	2003–2005
	Restructuring	Study on restructuring in candidate countries	2003–2005
	Lifelong learning	Include candidate countries in follow- up to framework of actions	2003–2004
	Implementation of legal acquis	Joint seminar on EWC	Seminar in 2004, inclusion in reporting 2005
	EU social and employment policies after enlargement	Prospective reflection to identify issues that will arise in the EU after enlargement such as increase in diversity, migration, transborder work, etc.	2004
Mobility	*Action plan on skills and mobility*	Seminar to identify areas where joint actions by the social partners at EU level could help address obstacles to mobility (notably for managerial staff), including supplementary pensions	Starting in 2004

Chapter Five
European Social Dialogue in Action: A Perspective from the UNICE

Wilfried Beirnaert

1. Before entering into the subject of the European social dialogue and looking at its possible evolution in the future, it seems important to me to place the social dialogue in a broader context, namely that of the European social model and of the remit of social Europe.

A European Social Model: Image Building or Reality?

2. The national social systems indisputably share some common features, but one cannot infer from this that there is a coherent and homogeneous European social model valid in all Member States.

Common Features

3. EU documents constantly refer to the European social model. The notion is rather woolly, but one cannot question the fact that the national social systems are marked by common features:

- the existence of employers' and workers' organizations acting as social partners able to negotiate agreements and considered as interlocutors by the public authorities;
- the fact that basic wage and labour conditions are largely covered by collective agreements;
- the existence of social protection systems providing a coverage for basic social risks, financed through solidarity levies;
- the existence of a network of social services.

National Specificity

4. The degree of implementation of these features, however, varies very largely according to the Member States. A few illustrations:

- the degree of unionization varies from nearly 8% in the private sector in France to more than 80% in Denmark;
- the coverage of labour conditions by collective agreements varies from 36% in the UK to more than 80% in the Scandinavian countries;
- the legal effects of collective agreements differ according to the Member States. Some countries know the technique of extension 'era omnes'; in the UK agreements are closer to gentlemen's agreements between the signatory parties;
- in most countries the sector prevails as the bargaining unit, but in some the plant level is predominant, and in others the national cross-industry level;
- as for social protection, the expenses vary from 16% of GNP in Ireland to 33% in Sweden;
- the way of financing and organizing social security varies widely according to the Member States.

The national social systems are so much determined by demographic, sociological, economic, political, historical and cultural factors that one can hardly state that there is a single coherent European social model. In contrast to the economy, which obeys to universal rules, social policy is much more marked by national specificities and sensitivities.

Some, however, distinguish different social models in Europe: the Scandinavian one, the Anglo-Saxon one, the Western-European one and the Mediterranean one. It cannot be questioned that some national systems bear more similarities, but I should not venture to deduce from this that they form social models. I dare even say that in the perspective of the entering the EMU, Member States have made different choices and have drifted apart. One can hardly say that Belgium and the Netherlands have taken the same path. Neither can one say that for Sweden and Finland.

The Remit of 'Social Europe'

5. As there is not a single European social model in the sense of a coherent and homogeneous blueprint valid for all Member States, the national level still prevails, but there is no denying that social Europe has progressively been built up as level of legislation, negotiation, dialogue, consultation and peer pressure, inspiration that the Member States have to take into account.

The Bulk of Social Competencies Still Rests With the Member States

6. Given the extent to which social Europe is rooted in a national context, it is not surprising that the bulk of social policy still rests with the Member

States. It is very significant that there is no field of action where the notion of subsidiarity is so closely watched as in the social field. It is very telling that the ongoing European convention largely agrees on strengthening the political and jurisdictional control in respect of the principle of subsidiarity.

The main areas of social policy remain essentially a national competence, either because they are shared competencies but subject to unanimity voting – social protection and social security, the collective defence of interests, including the industrial relations systems – or because they are complementary competencies where the EU has a supportive role, as for instance employment policy, education and training, and public health systems.

Normative Competencies at EU Level

7. The treaty of Maastricht has broadened the scope of matters subject to qualified majority voting at EU level. Before Maastricht it was restricted to security and health at the work place; Maastricht has extended the QMV to labour conditions and to information and consultation of the workers. As important as the extension of the QMV was that in parallel, the possibility was granted to the social partners to act as alternative legislators by concluding agreements. Two ways were opened: either the agreement would be endorsed by a directive, or the agreement should be implemented according to national mechanisms and practices. There are three examples of the first route – parental leave, part-time work and fixed-term contracts – and one recent example of the second route – the agreement on teleworking.

Will social Europe in the sense of a legislation and bargaining unit expand in the future? There is certainly still room for normative provisions or agreements in order to counter distortions of competition or to privilege basic values as the principle of non-discrimination, but I don't perceive a token of a political consensus on a significant transfer of normative competencies from the national to the EU level. The basic question, which is too often sidelined, is whether we will be better off with more European normative competencies. I doubt it, because Europe is a too large unit to integrate the contextual approach of social policy. I can only quote such a non-suspect person as Jacques Delors, the former chair of the EU commission, who stated '*doivent demeurer de la compétence exclusive des Etats: la politique de l'emploi, la sécurité sociale, la santé, la culture et l'éducation*'.

The Open Method of Co-ordination

8. Does that mean that Europe has no role to play in the field of employment, social protection, and training? On the contrary, but in my view not by means of harmonization or approximation, but by promoting convergence in fields where the competence of the national Member States still prevails. **It means that the mechanism of the open method of co-ordination, privileged by the summit of Lisbon, becomes increasingly a pre-eminent tool of social Europe.** It enables the EU to set down objectives, to oblige the Member States to elaborate national action plans, to define indicators, even to address recommendations to the Member States, but without prejudice to their normative competence.

A first example 'avant la lettre' were the guidelines for employment; the objectives for social inclusion followed, later came general objectives for sustainable pensions, and the commission favours the method of co-ordination for training, for immigration and asylum. The content of the method necessarily varies according to the dossiers, but the common denominator is to promote convergence while respecting national diversity.

WHICH PERSPECTIVE FOR THE EUROPEAN SOCIAL DIALOGUE?

9. A decade after the Maastricht summit the diagnosis is clear. The context has changed and will further change in the future. Therefore, the European social partners will have to adapt to the evolution. It is the rationale behind the joint declaration of the social partners to the Laeken summit (Dec. 2001).

Elements of Change

10. Different elements have reshuffled the cards:

- the switch to the economic and monetary union and the single currency;
- the increasing use of the open method of co-ordination, as already mentioned;
- the multiplying of tripartite consultation forums;
- the debate on the European governance implying the need for better consultation;
- in the wake of this the greater involvement of the organized civil society encroaching on the social dialogue.

New elements will emerge in the following years:

- The **institutional changes** we are heading for. What conclusions will the European convention, which must end its work in June 2003, draw in view of the next intergovernmental conference? Will the repartition of competencies in the social field between the EU and national level be changed? Will the EU competencies subject to unanimity voting be switched to qualified majority voting? Will the European parliament have a greater say in the social field by means of extension of its co-decision powers? What consequences will the integration of the charter of fundamental rights in the treaty have in terms of legal effects? Will the principle of the open method of co-ordination be enshrined in the Treaty? In which conditions? Will the principle of the consultation of the civil society be laid down in the Treaty? Will the pre-eminence of the social dialogue be confirmed in the Treaty, as requested by both social partners?

For the time being it is premature to answer those questions, as the European convention has just set up a working group on social Europe and entrusted it with the task to prepare an answer on those questions.

– How will the **enlargement of the EU** to 10 new Member States affect the social dialogue? In these countries, national bipartite social dialogue is still in a stage of apprenticeship. The tripartite dialogue still prevails with governments sitting in the driver's seat. Most applicant countries still lack an appropriate legislation on collective bargaining.

The Laeken Declaration

11. Fully aware of this changing context, the European social partners addressed a common declaration to the European summit in Laeken (December 2001).

In this declaration, they stressed the specificity of the social dialogue. *The nature of the responsibilities of the social partners, their legitimacy and their representativeness, together with their capacity to negotiate agreements, places the social dialogue in a special position.* They advocated a better conceptualization of social dialogue distinguishing bipartite social dialogue from tripartite concentration.

To prove their capacity of autonomy the social partners announced the drafting of a common work programme. This work programme would be built on a spectrum of diversified instruments (various types of European framework agreement, opinions, recommendations, statements, exchanges of experience, awareness-raising campaigns, open debates) and would comprise a balanced range of themes of common interest for employers and workers. This is for me a sentence of paramount importance. It means that if the social dialogue will gain more autonomy and will open the range of items, it will have to diversify the tools. The past has indeed shown that a social dialogue too focussed on the negotiation of compulsory agreements will inevitably be stuck.

A Joint Working Programme

12. The summit of the European social dialogue which met on November 28th approved a joint working programme for the period 2003–2005.

Through this ratification, the social partners sent a strong signal to the European convention emphasizing their will to take their full responsibility.

The programme provides a series of actions of different kinds, grouped around three priorities: employment, mobility and enlargement in order to acquaint the social partners of the applicant countries with the European social dialogue. The priority devoted to employment and mobility aspects is inspired by the will of the social partners to contribute to the implementation of the so-called Lisbon strategy (March 2000). According to this strategy Europe must for the next decade *become the most competitive and dynamic knowledge-based economy in the world capable of sustainable economic growth with more and better jobs and greater social cohesion.*

In this spirit the programme provides notably joint actions with regard to:

- lifelong learning;
- gender equality;
- young people;
- ageing workforce;
- restructuring;
- stress at work and harassment.

This programme deals with the bipartite aspects of social dialogue that the social partners want to treat autonomously; it does not cover the whole remit of the social dialogue in the broad sense. Besides the bipartite social dialogue, there will be many tripartite rendez-vous. The most striking example will be the social summit for growth and employment that the commission proposes to set up to replace the standing committee on employment. Another example is the contacts with the committee on social protection.

A crucial element will be the attitude that the European institutions will adopt vis-à-vis an autonomous programme. The social partners have enough realpolitik to know that this programme will not tie the European institutions up in their eagerness to occupy the social scene. If the European institutions however stick to their natural tendency to patronize the social dialogue, the implementation of the autonomous programme will be endangered.

Part Three
Community Institutions

Chapter Six
Challenges and Prospects for the European Social Dialogue

Michèle Thozet

The Challenges

1. The social dialogue is faced with unprecedented challenges at this time. First, the Lisbon European Council decided to take a single, comprehensive approach to economic, structural and employment initiatives; it also established strategic objectives for the next ten years. Those aims, attaining full employment and reinforcing social cohesion, are based largely on action by the social partners at all levels. In addition, the discussions on the future of Europe, launched by the White Paper on European governance, are not without consequences for the social partners. Their active involvement in the Union's decision-making process needs to be intensified, thanks, in particular, to greater consultation. This is especially important in the run-up to enlargement: independent social partnership in the candidate countries remains relatively weak and this is bound to have repercussions on governance in the future enlarged Union. Enlargement is therefore a major challenge for the social dialogue now that the candidate countries are on the Community threshold.

The Commission Communication

2. The Commission is fully aware of its responsibilities under the Treaty, which include the task of promoting and organizing the social dialogue, so it met these challenges by adopting a Communication on 26 June 2002. It was based on the deliberations of a High-Level Group (called the Rodrigues Group after its chairman) which brought together industrial relations experts and players, and on the social partners' contribution to the Laeken Summit in December 2001.

In that contribution, the social partners defined a framework for a new stage in the social dialogue. The framework encompasses strengthening and rationalizing tripartite concertation within a single forum, the Tripartite Social Summit for Growth and Employment, and enhancing their own bipartite social dialogue through adoption of a multiannual work programme.

Let me run through the broad lines of that approach.

Reinforcing the Role of the Social Partners in European Governance

3. The work and consultations in progress on improving governance when decisions are at the preparatory stage bear witness to the enormous demand for participation by civil society. And within civil society, the social partners hold a unique position, for they have a special role to play in issues connected with the world of work, for example, working conditions, continuing training and work organization.

The social partners are now able to make a practical contribution at European level to improving governance.

Thanks to the consultation processes in place, they can have their say before decisions are taken. The Commission thus consults the European social partners on the guidelines for and follow-up to the European employment strategy and on the future of pensions and health care.

Under Article 138 of the Treaty the social partners can negotiate in certain fields and ultimately draw up agreements which become European rules. This was the case, for example, with parental leave, fixed-term contracts and part-time work. This highly innovative form of joint regulation ensures balance and effectiveness.

The Commission supports this approach to consultation and provides backing in its Communication for means to extend it.

Reinforcing the Social Partners' Bipartite Contribution

4. In line with the conclusions of the Rodrigues Group, the Commission believes that the social dialogue can constitute a tool for the modernization announced at the Lisbon European Council of all the key items on the European Social Agenda which gave shape to the strategy defined in Lisbon. At present, the social partners' bipartite contribution is developed within the cross-industry social dialogue and 27 sectoral social dialogue committees.

In its Communication, the Commission urged the social partners to move forward on two fronts.

Firstly, it called on them to prepare *multiannual work programmes*, setting out the topics they wish to deal with in the social dialogue and the objectives set. A programme will be presented at a social dialogue summit in the near future.

This step, which the social partners announced at Laeken, will enable the social dialogue to contribute, not merely to react, to the discussions in hand.

Recent progress, for example, the adoption last March in Barcelona of a 'framework of actions for the lifelong development of competences and qualifications' and the opening, this week, of discussions on anticipating change and managing restructuring, are strong signs of this new approach in the European dialogue, with its own, independent dynamic.

5. Against that background, the Commission is encouraging the social partners to extend and enhance their dialogue by expanding the scope of the negotiations. The social dialogue can come up with appropriate responses, bringing new kinds of flexibility and security to the issues at stake today, such as the development of lifelong learning, active ageing, social inclusion, and the promotion of equal opportunities and diversity.

In addition, the Commission is requesting the social partners to include new ways and means in its operations by drawing inspiration from the lessons learnt and practices of the *open method of coordination* defined in Lisbon and by concluding voluntary agreements. The agreement on telework, signed at cross-industry level on 16 July last, will be the first agreement of this kind implemented in accordance with the social partners' own procedures and practices. This is the first time that an agreement concluded at cross-industry level will no longer be implemented by means of a Council directive as was the case with parental leave, part-time employment and fixed-term contracts.

Reorganizing the Tripartite Arenas at European Level

6. The Communication also tackles the question of the links established over time between the social partners and the European institutions in the context of tripartite concertation. Initially introduced in the late 60s and early 70s in cross-industry advisory committees, in the Standing Committee on Employment and tripartite conferences, tripartite concertation has been extended in more recent years to cover many more topics with the launch of the employment strategy, the setting in place of the macroeconomic dialogue, the work on social protection and the follow-up to the Lisbon European Council.

In each of these areas, the dialogue between the Commission, the Member States and the social partners takes place in different forums at different times. The social summits organized in March 2001 in Stockholm and in March 2002 in Barcelona demonstrated the need for integrated dialogue at the highest level.

In their joint contribution to the Laeken summit, the social partners maintained that concertation should be reviewed to improve consistency between the different processes with which they are associated.

The proposal to establish a Tripartite Social Summit for Growth and Employment, now under discussion in the Council and the European Parliament, will enable the social partners to put forward a contribution within a single forum before each spring European Council. And this contribution will be an integral part of the follow-up to the Lisbon strategy.

CONCLUSIONS

7. The European social dialogue has arrived at a crossroads. It has considerable scope for action. To take on its role properly at European level, it needs to broaden its practices, diversify its operational methods and use to best advantage the entire bargaining area.

We are about to break new ground in the development of the European social dialogue and the social partners' contribution. We have an important rendezvous on 28 November next, a bipartite social dialogue summit; this meeting should bring us forward into a new era with the adoption of the social partners' multiannual work programme.

Chapter Seven
Social Dialogue, a Cornerstone of our European Social Model

Jos Bertrand and MEP Anne Van Lancker

Introduction

1. The social dialogue is one of the cornerstones of our social model. Obviously this did not happen overnight: we must realize that it is a product of 100 years of evolution in our Member States and that in each of our countries the rules and practices vary widely. Social dialogue as it operates now is the result of a longstanding process, which has evolved from the mere confrontation between both sides of enterprises to real partnerships, based on mutual recognition.

This system has been introduced now at the European level and must also become a cornerstone of our European social model. However the Europeanization of social dialogue is relatively new, being launched only in 1985, with a lack of practice at European level and without strong Europe-wide organization of trade unions or employers before this. The articles 138 and 139 in the 1992 Maastricht Treaty establishing the legal framework for Europe-wide collective agreements and consultation, were a joint proposal of ETUC, UNICE and CEEP, which are organized at European level as federations of trade unions, industries or public services, representing the largest organizations from the Member States.

2. In the Member States, social dialogue applies to a wide range of subjects. At Union level large industries have de facto long been involved in the conception of European policy in economic (common market regulations) and in social issues; trade unions are only involved in social policy issues. The realization of the economic and monetary union (EMU) calls for the deepening of the European social dialogue concept, while economic and monetary decisions taken at EU level have important repercussion on the social dialogue in the Member States. It also has consequences for the financing of social security schemes, investment policy and salaries. Since 1997, social dialogue at EU level has gain importance, but basically – as

Commission documents indicated – has focussed on industrial change or employment measures. Social concertation on macro-economic issues is of a much more recent date (1999), and is not widely accepted.

Much remains to be done if we want effectively to install social dialogue at the European level. In view of the enlargement of the Union with 12 new Member States, which have a weak tradition of social dialogue, this entails an immense challenge, not only for the architecture of social dialogue and concertation in Europe, but also for the relationship between social partners.

Four European Collective Agreements: The Result from 10 Years After Maastricht?

3. From 1993 till now, only 4 collective agreements have been negotiated at European level based on article 138 and 139 of the Treaty: parental leave (1995), temporary work (1997), part-time work (1997) and telework (2002). Other negotiations have resulted in 1 common opinion (European Works Council), 6 separate opinions, and 1 failure (on temporary work). The fourth collective agreement on telework will not be transposed into a directive and shall also have no binding effect. Frankly speaking, these results do not reflect good social relationships.

The problem is that at European level, there is no appropriate power balance between trade unions and employer organizations. ETUC is a federation of trade unions, which are basically oriented towards their own state. There is no tradition of Europe-wide organization. The action of the trade unions in 1997 following the closure of the Renault Vilvoorde plant was the first sign of Europe-wide action from trade unions in a labour conflict. Even though ETUC is co-ordinating action at EU level with regard to political or social issues and mobilization is growing, this is not enough to build a more balanced powerful relation between social partners in Europe. On the other side, UNICE is not very enthusiastic about binding social regulation. They argue for co-ordination, codes of conduct, for soft regulation, but against what they call 'harmonization'. They also use the subsidiarity principle, saying that social and labour matters are too different and too complex for harmonization and that the most appropriate level for labour regulation is the company level. The fact that there is no consensus amongst social partners to request transposition of the tele-work agreement is a bad signal.

4. In July 2002, in its resolution on the implementation of the social agenda, the European parliament called for more active participation by the social partners, and in particular employers, in the attainment of the objectives set, particularly with regard to lifelong education and training, work organization and adaptation to new forms of work, and the need to strike a balance between professional and private life. The Parliament considers that the Commission should submit legislative instruments whenever negotiations between social partners are not concluded within a reasonable period.

The European Parliament was critical about the dispositions of articles 138–139 because Europe-wide collective agreements can be declared generally binding by the Council only, acting on a proposal from the Commission, without any involvement of the European Parliament, and that the European Council has to decide unanimously about European collective agreements with regard to protection of workers where their employment contract is terminated, representation and collective defence of the interests of workers and employers, including co-determination and conditions of employment for third-country nationals legally residing in Community territory. We must also recognize that a democratic gap exists due to the fact that if social partners are not able, or willing, to fulfil their responsibility, Parliament cannot create pressure, while only the Commission can propose regulation.

NON-BINDING AGREEMENT, CONSULTATION IN ADVISORY COMMITTEES AND COMMON POSITIONS

5. The recent Communication of the Commission, proposing the creation of a Tripartite Social Summit, also foresees social dialogue and consultations of the social partners within advisory committees or in the context of procedures aimed at gathering the views of interested parties, for example, through Green papers. The Commission Communication mentioned health and safety at work, vocational training, equal opportunities, freedom of movement and social security for migrant workers, but also systematic consultation on implementation reports.

The Commission also mentioned 230 common positions issued by sectoral social partners – existing in 17 industrial sectors – and 40 common positions at Europe-wide level. But the Commission mentioned that in most cases, these texts did not include any provision for implementation and monitoring, and were responses to short-term concerns. They are not well known and their dissemination at national level has been limited.

Their effectiveness is thus disputable. This is not merely due to lack of transparency or publicity, as the Commission suggested. There is a need not only to strengthen networking and co-ordination between different levels of policy making (local, regional, national, European), but also to have more concrete results, having effect on the local and company level, affecting the daily life of workers and companies.

What is also true is that when European agreements are transposed, workers and companies must be informed that it is the execution of a decision taken at European level.

European Works Council

6. European social dialogue at company level is also an important issue with regard to industrial changes. It is important to mention that it took about 25 years to reach a compromise on the European Works Councils directive of 1994; after that the Maastricht Treaty, providing in a qualified majority decision in the Council and co-decision in this matter, came into force (October 1993). Success is growing: in 2002 the Commission reported 800 EWC as compared to 650 mentioned in the implementation report of 2000. But it is a relative success, since over 1800 companies are covered by this directive. It means that half of the Europe-wide large companies do not have a Europe-wide works council.

In any case, this directive contains some really weak elements, as was illustrated by the closure of the Renault Vilvoorde plant. Key problems are the lack of adequate sanctions in case of non-compliance and the protection of workers' representatives. The European Parliament was successful in introducing the revision of the 1994 Directive in the European Social Agenda, which was approved in December 2000 by the Employment and Social Affairs Council, and thus added this point on the Commission proposal.

As revision of the Directive is planned for 2003, the European Parliament is pressing the Commission to propose a revised directive strengthening the EWC. In its resolution on the Commission report on the application of the European works council directive from September 2001, the Parliament reiterates its call on the Commission to submit a proposal for the revision of the directive in order to ensure that information and consultation takes place in good time and at regular intervals before the decision by the company or group management, so as to allow the employees genuinely to influence the management's decision-making process and to lower the thresholds for companies to be included within the scope of the directive from 1000 to 500 employees for the company as a whole and from 150 to 100 employees per establishment in at least two Member States. The Parliament also asks that decisions of central management or any other management level shall be valid only if information and consultation are properly carried out, with due regard for the principles of confidentiality of the information. The Parliament also argues for the suppression of article 13 from the Directive, which allows the maintenance of weaker information and consultation structures if these were already agreed before the date of implementation of the Directive. Parliament also requests reinforcement of the protection of the workers' representatives.

Social Concertation on Economic and Employment Issues

7. Since 1997 social concertation at bipartite and at tripartite level has been strengthened. The Amsterdam Treaty refers to the social partners in the chapter on Employment (article 130) as bodies to be consulted by the Employment Committee. The Resolution on Employment, which is an element from the Stability and Growth Pact, issued by the Amsterdam Summit, also gives a limited role to social partners with regard to social-economic issues.

Social partners and social dialogue at European level have become more and more important, not only in the economic co-ordination and in employment strategy, but also in the implementation and the follow-up of the 2000–2005 European Social Agenda and the so-called 'Lisbon strategy'. The 1997 Employment Summit led to the establishment of a so-called 'social Summit' between social partners and Presidency Troika of the Union. The 1999 Köln Summit established the macro-economic dialogue between Member States, social partners, Commission and the European Central Bank. This macro-economic dialogue is an embryo for Europe-wide social-economical governance. It can become an instrument for a more balanced approach to pay-policy, which is not a competence of the Union: indeed, it belongs to a no-go area (article 137.6). The March 2000 Lisbon European Summit issued the 'open method of co-ordination', which also provides an opportunity for involvement of social partners into the co-ordination on social exclusion and on pensions. Many issues of social dialogue go much further than the policy areas mentioned into the social chapter of the Treaty.

The Convention on the Future of the Union: an Opportunity to Strengthen Social Dialogue

8. The Convention is an opportunity to try to reinforce the existing dispositions in the Treaty and to integrate new practices and European Summit conclusions about the involvement of social partners in European policy. What can be proposed?

1. Whereas the Treaty gives responsibility for promoting social dialogue to the Commission, this obligation should be strengthened in the new Constitution. A distinction must be made between three types of dialogue: tripartite social dialogue (cf. preparation for the Spring summits, macro-economic dialogue), social dialogue between autonomous partners as co-legislator (cf article 138–139), which requires a procedure for binding (erga omnes) declarations, and social dialogue as platform for preparing policy and consultation.
2. Social dialogue has to be introduced in the Constitution, as it is a cornerstone of our social and democratic model and an instrument for pursuing the respect of fundamental rights and the missions of the Union. Social dialogue should not just be confined to the fields covered by the social chapter, but could also cover initiatives to combat discrimination, education and vocational training and aspects of immigration policy. A 'blanket' article in the Constitutional Treaty should enable the Commission to consult management and labour on any matter that concerns them and to promote social dialogue. The fact that the skeleton for a Constitution, presented by the Presidium of the Convention in October 2002, provided a separate Charter VI on the 'democratic life of the Union' is a good opportunity to argues in this sense.
3. I know that the social partners are not in favour of re-opening the discussion about articles 138 and 139 of the Treaty. These articles are the result of social dialogue discussions before the Maastricht Summit. On the other hand, it is clear that the procedure for collective agreements can be made stronger. As social agreement is a result of autonomous social partners' dialogue, it could be better to anticipate a Council decision about generally binding effect by qualified majority and to give the Commission the task of checking on representativeness before the Council declares it generally binding. This implies that the Commission investigates whether all actors concerned have been properly involved in the negotiation leading to an agreement. This should avoid the European Court of Justice ever again being asked to 'annul' an agreement. A Court is not the best-situated institution to take such a task on board.
4. Whereas Treaty denies the Union competence in respect of wage policy, even though the Union has exclusive competence for defining monetary policy, and the annual Broad Economic Policy Guidelines give guidance on labour cost issues, which ultimately influences the definition of wage policy and the corresponding negotiations, it would be wise, while respecting the autonomous position of the social partners, to concede the possibility of wage agreements at a European level. The exclusion

of Community competence, particularly over pay, the right of association and the right to strike, must also thus be abolished.

5. In order to facilitate social partners' participation in economic policy, the necessary institutional framework needs to be created.
   - An independent bipartite social dialogue committee (a 'European Labour Council') should be created as proposed by the High level group on industrial relations.
   - The December 2001 Laeken Summit suggested the creation of a tripartite Social Summit, which should be involved in the preparation of the co-ordination of the economic, employment and social policy in preparation of the so-called Spring Summits. The European Commission laid down a proposal to this effect on June 26. This proposal seems very minimalist. Nevertheless it met a lot of resistance in the Council, and discussion focussed on technical and legal problems and Community competencies. Also the new Constitution can create a legal basis for such an instrument. In order to increase the input of social partners, not only (macro-) economic policy, employment policy and the co-ordination of social policy, but also the macro-economic dialogue, should be formalized within the framework of this Tripartite Committee for Social Dialogue on Growth, Employment and Social Cohesion.
   - To strengthen the social partners' involvement into economic and monetary policy, an advisory committee on the ECB – as existing in Belgium – can be suggested.
   - Also, a genuine system of industrial relations should allow for recourse to mediation and arbitration procedures if conflicts rise.
6. Last but not least, a disposition must be introduced in the new Constitution providing for the exclusion of the rules of competition from agreements made between management and labour in accordance with the social objectives (Article 81). Even European competition policy challenges national, regional or sectorial social agreements which relate to financing education projects in industrial sectors, while financial support from employers or employees which are part of social security payments are interpreted as state aid. This is an issue that shows how economic policy impedes the objectives of the employment policy co-ordination in the European Union, and it also needs to be solved.

List of publications in this series

STUDIES IN EMPLOYMENT AND SOCIAL POLICY

1. W. Beck, L. van der Maesen and A. Walker (eds.): *The Social Quality of Europe*. 1997. ISBN: 90411 0456 9
2. F. Pennings: *Introduction to European Social Security Low*. 2001. ISBN: 90411 1628 1
3. R. Blanpain, M. Colucci, C. Engels, F. Hendrickx, L. Salas and J. Wouters: *Institutional Changes and European Social Policies after the Treaty of Amsterdam*. 1998. ISBN: 90411 1018 6
4. Vai Jo Lo: *Low and Industrial Relations: China and Japan after World War II*. 1998. ISBN: 90 411 1075 5
5. A. Den Exter and H. Hermans (eds.): *The Right to Health Care in Several European Countries*. 1998. ISBN: 90 411 1087 9
6. M. Biagi (ed.): *Job Creation and Labour Law. from Protection towards Pro-action*. 2000. ISBN: 90 411 1432 7
7. W. Beck, L.J.G. van der Maesen, F. Thomése and A. Walker (eds.): *Social Quality: a Vision for Europe*. 2000. ISBN: 90 411 1523 4
8. J. Murray: *Transnational Labour Regulation: The ILO and EC Compared*. 2001. ISBN: 90 411 183 8
9. R. Blanpain and C. Engels (eds.): *The ILO and Social Challenges of the 21st century*. 2001. ISBN: 90 411 1572 2
10. M. Biagi (ed.): *Towards a European Model of Industrial Relations?* 2001. ISBN: 90 411 1653 2
11. J. Clasen (ed.): *What Future for Social Security? Debates and Reforms in National and Cross-National Perspective*. 2001. ISBN: 90 411 1671 0
12. A. Numhauser Hennings (ed.): *Legal Perspectives on Equal Treatment and Non Discrimination*. 2001. ISBN: 90 411 1665 6
13. R. Blanpain (ed.): *Labour Law, Human Rights and Social Justice*. 2001. ISBN: 90 411 1697 4
14. M-C. Kuo, HF. Zacher and H-S. Chan (eds.): *Reform and Perspectives on Social Insurance: Lessons from the East and West*. 2002. ISBN: 90 411 1842 x
15. P. Foubert: *The Legal Protection of the Pregnant Worker in the European Commu nity*. 2002. ISBN: 90 411 1842 x
16. M. Biagi (ed.): *Quality of Work and Employee Involvement in Europe*. 2002. ISBN: 90 411 1885 3
17. F. Pennings: *Dutch Social Security Law in an International Context*. 2002. ISBN: 90 411 1887 x
18. T. Carney and G Ramia: *From Rights to Management: Contract, New Public Management and Employment Services*. 2002. ISBN: 90 411 1889 6
19. R. Blanpain and M. Colucci: *European Labour and Social Security Law, Glossary*. 2002. ISBN: 90 411 1905 1

20. I.U. Zeytinoğlu (ed.): *Flexible Work Arrangements. Conceptualizations and International Experiences.* 2002. ISBN: 90 411 1947 7
21. J. Berghman, A. Nagelkerke, K. Boos, R. Doeschot and G Vonk (eds.): *Social Security in Transition.* 2002. ISBN: 90 411 1969 8
22. R. Blanpain: *The Legal Status of Sportsmen and Sportswomen under International, European and Belgian National and Regional Law.* 2003. ISBN: 90 411 1980 9
23. R. Blanpain and M. Weiss (eds.): *Changing Industrial Relations & Modernisation of Labour Law, Liber Amicorum in Honour of Professor Marco Biagi.* 2003. ISBN: 90 411 2008 4
24. J. Malmberg (ed.), B. Fitzpatrick, M. Gotthardt, S. Laulom, A. Lo Faro, T. van Peijpe, A. Swiatkowski: *Effective Enforcement of EC Labour Law.* 2003. ISBN: 90 411 2160 9
25. M. De Vos (ed.): *A Decade Beyond Maastricht: The European Social Dialogue Revisited.* 2003. ISBN: 90 411 2190 0